Figure Skating Today

THE NEXT WAVE OF STARS

Qing Pang/Jian Tong

Figure Skating Today

THE NEXT WAVE OF STARS

Steve Milton

Photographs by Gérard Châtaigneau

FIREFLY BOOKS

A FIREFLY BOOK

Published by Firefly Books Ltd. 2007

First printing

Publisher Cataloging-in-Publication Data (U.S.)

Milton, Steve.
    Figure skating today : the next wave of stars / Steve Milton ; photographs by Gérard Châtaigneau.
[   ] p. : col. photos. ;   cm.
Includes index.
Summary: Focusing on the stars of the 2006-2007 figure skating season, events covered include: the Grand Prix Final, the Canadian, American and Japanese Nationals, the European Figure Skating Championships, Four Continents Figure Skating Championships, Junior World Championships, World Synchronized Skating Championships, and the World Championships in Tokyo.
ISBN-13: 978-1-55407-335-1 (pbk.)
ISBN-10: 1-55407-335-9 (pbk.)
1. Figure skaters. 2. Figure skating—Tournaments. I. Châtaigneau, Gérard. II. Title.
796.912 dc22   GV850.4.M558 2007

Library and Archives Canada Cataloguing in Publication

Milton, Steve
    Figure skating today : the next wave of stars / Steve
Milton ; photographs by Gérard Châtaigneau.

Includes index.
ISBN-13: 978-1-55407-335-1
ISBN-10: 1-55407-335-9

    1. Skaters. 2. Skating. I. Châtaigneau, Gérard II. Title.

GV850.A2M533 2007   796.91'20922   C2007-902683-4

Published in the United States by
Firefly Books (U.S.) Inc.
P.O. Box 1338, Ellicott Station
Buffalo, New York 14205

Published in Canada by
Firefly Books Ltd.
66 Leek Crescent
Richmond Hill, Ontario L4B 1H1

Cover and interior design by Kimberley Young.

Printed in Canada

The publisher gratefully acknowledges the financial support for our publishing program by the Government of Canada through the Book Publishing Industry Development Program.

Cover: *Mao Asada*
Back Cover: *(top to bottom) Marie-France Dubreuil and Patrice Lauzon, Miki Ando, Marigold Ice Unity, Xue Shen and Hongbo Zhao, Stéphane Lambiel*

Contents

Miki Ando

Introduction

Miki Ando, the final skater of the season, stared up at the scoreboard, her face in a state of suspended animation. While the crowd clapped in unsion, she hung frozen between exhausted relief and whatever would happen next.

Suddenly her marks, the last scores of the year, appeared in an electronic flash: personal bests of 125.85 points in the freeskate, and 195.09 overall. Beneath them, the most important number of her young life. In Japanese: *iti*. In English: *one*. Universal translation: *world champion*.

As the reality struck her, Ando broke into syncopated sobs, and she pressed both hands to her face, a rivulet of tears streaking first one cheek, then the other. The 19-year-old jumping pioneer hugged her coach Nikolai Morozov so hard, she drenched his dark suit coat. She could not control her crying, even as she was being interviewed on the spot for the benefit of the crammed stands at the Tokyo Metropolitan Gymnasium. She tried to answer a question and would get only a few words out before the tears would force her to take a deep breath.

Less than a year after her controversial selection to the Japanese Olympic team, subsequent 15th-place finish and being roasted in the national press, Miki Ando was the champion of the most anticipated event at the most important world championship ever held in Japan. She had beaten the two sensational 16 year olds who dominated all the pre-Worlds attention, teammate Mao Asada and South Korea's Yu-Na Kim. And now that the almost unbearable pressure was over — if only to be reborn again, like a perennial flower, in a few weeks — her tears, of joy and of remembered pain, released it.

"I did not expect that I could win," she said through tears.

In figure skating, there are always tears.

That's half the reason they call the area where skaters wait for their marks the Kiss 'n' Cry. And there's usually a lot more cryng than kissing.

Top to bottom: Miki Ando, Mao Asada, Daisuke Takahashi

JPN

Daisuke Takahashi

Born: March 16, 1986

Hometown: Okayama, Japan

Training sites: Osaka, Japan; Simsbury, Connecticut

Coach: Utako Nagamitusu

Choreographer: Nikolai Morozov

- Won freeskate at 2007 Worlds to finish 2nd, best ever by a Japanese man

- 2nd, Grand Prix Final 2007; 1st, NHK, 2006; 2nd, Skate Canada, 2006

- Won world junior title in first appearance (2002)

- Moved to Osaka for college in 2004. School built a new rink, where he trains

- Influenced by Takeshi Honda and Olympic champs Alexei Yagudin and Evgeni Plushenko

But the 2007 world championship, which confirmed a dramatic eastward shift in skating's power balance, was an even wetter Worlds than most. There was more spontaneous emotion among the winners, and there will continue to be more as the sport heads to Vancouver's 2010 Olympics. That's because skaters can no longer absolutely expect a certain result. They cannot prepare their body language or their victory speech in advance, because there is no understood and accepted pecking order. You must skate, and skate well, on the day — or you will lose. When skaters do perform well, and do win, they are drained to exhaustion with no defense against overwhelming feelings.

Forty-eight hours before Ando's emotional celebration, there had been an even more graphic spilling of tears. Daisuke Takahashi, Ando's mercurial countryman, won the freeskate to capture the silver medal, the best finish by a Japanese man in the history of the world championships. Overcome by the magnitude of the performance of his life, he sobbed uncontrollably for several minutes, as the partisan crowd cheered lustily, smashing the old stereotype of the quietly appreciative Japanese audience. Takahashi had played to the crowd, and the crowd to him.

"I heard the roaring cheers from the audience when I was getting tired, so I just tried to respond and complete the program," he said.

What a response. He landed a quad, with a slight touch of the hand to the ice — his only mistake in four-and-a-half minutes of dynamic brilliance — and eight triples. At the end, amid the deafening applause, he could not contain himself, and broke down.

Once again, the human towel was Nikolai Morozov, who works with both Ando and Takahashi, and dozens of others, half a world away in Simsbury, Connecticut.

The night before Takahashi's tearful reaction, observant fans could detect a dew drop or two on

JPN

Miki Ando

Born: December 18, 1987

Hometown: Nagoya City, Japan

Training site: Hackensack, New Jersey

Coaches: Yuko Monna; Nikolai Morozov

Choreographer: Nikolai Morozov

- Won world championships in 2007

- In 2006–07: 5th, Grand Prix Final; 2nd, Skate America; 2nd, Trophée Eric Bompard

- 4th at 2004 Worlds, 6th in 2005

- Landed the first quad jump by a woman (Salchow, 2002 Junior Grand Prix Final)

- Three-time world junior medalist (bronze, 2002; silver, 2003; gold, 2004)

- 15th at the 2006 Olympics, then left off the Japanese world team a month later; moved to New Jersey to work with Morozov, turning career around

the normally impassive face of coach Bin Yao. The architect of China's wall of dominance in the pairs discipline, Yao was a member the first pairs team to represent China 27 years earlier, and he had been humiliated by a lack of preparation and an inability to compete. When his exemplary students Xue Shen

C H N

Xue Shen and Hongbo Zhao

PAIRS

Born: November 13, 1978;
September 22, 1973

Hometown: Harbin, China

Training site: Beijing, China

Coach: Bin Yao

Choreographer: Lori Nichol

- Xue and Hongbo, considered among the greatest pairs of all time, won 3rd world title in 2007

- In 2006–07: 1st at Cup of China, NHK, Grand Prix Final, Four Continents, Asian Games

- Won China's first Worlds pairs title in 2002, their 10th season together

- Taking 2007–08 off; may return for Vancouver Olympics

- Made stirring recovery from his Achilles tendon rupture to win bronze at 2006 Olympics

and Hongbo Zhao skated off the ice and likely into retirement, with their third world championship and a long, loving, standing ovation, Yao shed a subtle tear. The awkward kids he had nurtured and driven for 15 difficult years were now mature adults, and they were leaving the Kiss 'n' Cry, probably for the last time. They were leaving as multiple champions, and their logical heirs were also Chinese: either 2006 world champions Qing Pang and Jian Tong, or daredevil youngsters Dan Zhang and Hao Zhang.

In 1980, as Bin Yao and Bo Luan made China's pairs debut at Worlds, their first of three consecutive last-place finishes, Asia had won just two world championship medals: bronzes by Japan's Emi Watanabe in 1979 and Minoru Sano two years earlier. But in 2007, two-thirds of the nine available medals in the men's, women's and pairs' events went to Asian countries: three to Japan, two to China, one to South Korea.

Bin Yao, who had been there for the worst, was now watching the best, Shen and Zhao, bid farewell. No wonder he was moved.

Skating to the Olympics

Historically, there has been a fairly predictable rhythm to those world championships staged between Olympics. The Worlds held the same year as an Olympics, however, were a sign-off for the old guard and a brief hint of what was to come: like Kurt Browning landing the planet's first quad in 1988. The world championships held the year after the Olympics involved a widespread sorting-out process, with veterans trying to assess whether it was worth staying at the grind for another three years, mid-range skaters frantically trying to move up the ladder, and newcomers vying to make a strong early impression that could lead to judging favor later on. The mid-Olympiad Worlds — which for Vancouver 2010 would equate to the 2008 event in Göteborg, Sweden — usually saw the main contenders rising to the top and beginning to square off directly against

Qing Pang and Jian Tong

PAIRS

Born: December 24, 1979; August 15, 1979

Hometown: Harbin, China

Training site: Beijing, China

Coach: Bin Yao

Choreographer: Wenyi Cong

- Were 2nd at Worlds in 2007; 1st in 2006 and 3rd in 2004
- In 2006–07: 2nd, Cup of China; 6th, Grand Prix Final; 2nd, Four Continents
- Have three well-spaced titles in tough Chinese Nationals (2000, '04, '07)
- Both were singles skaters, and he also took up dance for two years

each other for the next 23 months. And the Worlds held just 11 months before an Olympics — this time at Los Angeles in 2009 — served to separate the haves from the have-nots entering the anxiety-laden fall season preceding February's Games.

But although a few elements of that pace remain, several important factors have radically

Brian Joubert

Dan Zhang/Hao Zhang

14

altered the beat. Everything is far less rigid than in the past. And never was this new direction more glaringly obvious than at the 2007 world championships in Tokyo, the first Worlds of the Vancouver Olympiad.

The new points-based International Judging System was instituted for the 2004–05 season to replace the century-old 6.0 marking grid that contributed heavily to the disastrous judging scandal at the 2002 Salt Lake City Olympics. Now, with each small segment of a program assessed a weighted value and judges forced to mark it immediately, it matters only what skaters do that day, not what they have done in the past or might do in the future.

The impact has been profound, producing a variety of leaders from event to event, and from short program to freeskate. The system encourages a more all-round skater who can jump, spin and unleash intricate footwork, all at high speed and with captivating choreography.

Powerful national associations can no longer directly influence judges, whose freedom to mark is protected by anonymity, random selection and internal review. Skaters who should score well, are scoring well.

So, although the 2006 champions in all four disciplines also competed at 2007 Worlds, none came in as prohibitive favorite; and only one, the Bulgarian ice dance team of Albena Denkova and Maxim Staviski, was able to repeat its gold. And Denkova and Staviski had entered the competition greatly disheartened, after plunging to third place at the European championships.

Men's 2006 champion Stéphane Lambiel dropped to third at Tokyo. His female counterpart, Kimmie Meissner, missed the podium completely, in fourth. The 2006 pairs winners, Qing Pang and Jian Tong, finished second, well behind the legendary Xue Shen and Hongbo Zhen who, over their 16-year career, had evolved from awkward, remote pioneers with gigantic tricks and little else into flowing, beloved idols.

BUL

Albena Denkova and Maxim Staviski

ICE DANCING

Born: December 3, 1974; November 16, 1977

Hometowns: Sofia, Bulgaria; Rostov, Russia

Training site: Newark, Delaware

Coaches: Natalia Linichuk, Gennadi Karpanosov

Choreographer: Natalia Linichuk

- Won their second successive Worlds ice dance title in 2007

- First Bulgarian skaters to win Worlds, and first to medal at Worlds (bronze, 2003)

- She is president of the Bulgarian Skating Federation; he grew up in Russia

- They are a couple on and off the ice

Any skating fans who had been completely out of contact with the sport for three years and returned to witness the 2007 Worlds would have thought they'd landed on the wrong planet. There were that many mold-smashing developments.

For the first time in 69 years, a country other than the United States (which had done it five times) finished one-two in the women's event.

JPN

Mao Asada

Born: September 25, 1990

Hometown: Nagoya City, Japan

Training site: Lake Arrowhead, California

Coach: Rafael Arutunian

Choreographer: Lori Nichol

- Stole the show, finishing 2nd in world championship debut in 2007

- In 2006–07: 2nd, Grand Prix Final; 1st, NHK; 3rd, Skate America

- Age-ineligible for Olympics and Worlds in 2006, despite great season

- 1st, Junior Worlds (2005); 2nd ('06)

- Landed her first triple Axels at 2005 Junior Grand Prix Final and Junior Worlds

- Sister Mai is two years older, and they both moved to California before 2006–07 season for more ice time

Japan's Miki Ando won the gold, but her 16-year-old teammate Mao Asada won the hearts, and the silver, with a brilliant freeskate, which left her just 0.64 points from gold. It was the first time in any discipline that Japan placed two skaters on the same podium, and it came just a year after another Japanese woman, Shizuka Arakawa, had given her country its first Olympic skating gold. Only one year earlier, Ando had been 15th at the Olympics, and because of the depth of women's skating in Japan, she was left off the 2006 world team completely.

The electric Yu-Na Kim's bronze medal performance won South Korea its first skating medal, giving Asia a sweep of the women's podium for the first time.

Two of the three women's medals were won by 16 year olds (Asada and Kim) who were competing in their first world championships and were too young to compete at the Olympics the season before. For the first time in 13 years, there was no American medalist in women's singles.

Brian Joubert, so often plagued by nerves and the tendency to reduce quads to triples, gave France its first men's title in 42 years. Alain Calmat,

 KOR

Yu-Na Kim

Born: September 5, 1990

Hometown: Gyounggi-Do, South Korea

Training site: Toronto, Ontario

Coach: Brian Orser

Choreographers: Tom Dickson; David Wilson

- Made Worlds debut in 2007, finishing 3rd
- First Worlds medal ever by Korean skater
- Spectacular 2006–07 season: Grand Prix Final champion; 1st, Trophée Eric Bompard; 3rd, Skate Canada
- World junior champion 2006; Junior Grand Prix Final champion 2005
- Silver at 2005 Junior Worlds — was first ISU medal ever by a Korean
- Privately tutored, she hasn't attended school in Korea for several years

Shizuka Arakawa

who won for France in 1965, was in attendance, as he was in 2004 when Joubert became the first Frenchman since Calmat to capture the European crown. "He has been the best skater in the world for years and he really deserves this," Calmat said. He also had to earn it.

Tanith Belbin/Ben Agosto

For the first time in 47 years, no skater from Russia or the former Soviet Union won a medal in any discipline. Moreover, in pairs, which they had completely dominated with 66 medals (32 of them gold) in the previous 42 years, there was only one Russian team in the top 10. Yuko Kawaguchi and Alexander Smirnov came ninth ... and she was raised and trained *in Japan*. This drought emphasized a decline in Russian skating that was predicted after the fall of communism in the early 1990s, but did not materialize until the new century. Given the massive country's historic ability to recover, and with a healthy financial climate for touring shows — which tend to inspire young athletes to take up

CAN

Marie-France Dubreuil and Patrice Lauzon

ICE DANCING

Born: August 11, 1974; November 26, 1975

Hometowns: Montreal, Quebec

Training site: Lyon, France

Coaches: Muriel Zazoui; Steffany Hanlen

Choreographers: David Wilson; Julie Marcotte

• Won silver at 2007 Worlds, just 1.15 points out of first

• Recovered from terrible fall at '06 Olympics to silver medal at 2006 Worlds, winning freedance and losing gold by 0.47 points

• Won fourth consecutive national title in 2007

• In 2006–07: 2nd, Grand Prix Final; 1st, Four Continents, Skate Canada, NHK

• Moved to Lyon after 2002 season

• Have delayed their wedding until after amateur career

Tessa Virtue/Scott Moir

figure skating — it would be unwise to count the Big Bear out.

Most shockingly, the only medals won by North Americans came in the continent's once barren division: the former European private preserve of ice dancing. Marie-France Dubreuil and Patrice Lauzon of Canada narrowly missed gold for the second straight year, and U.S. champions Tanith Belbin and Ben Agosto completed a frustrating season of struggling with their freedance, to take bronze. Accenting the increasingly blurred borders of big-time figure skating, of those four only Agosto trains in the country where he was born — and he is the only one who didn't grow up in Canada.

Moreover, four of the top seven dance teams were North American. By far the hottest new

Meryl Davis/Charlie White

couples making their world debuts were Canadians Tessa Virtue and Scott Moir, who finished sixth; and their former Juniors rivals, Americans Meryl Davis and Charlie White, just four points back in seventh. Just as Asian women and men are starting to dominate like never before, partly because of a more equitable judging system and international coaching, so are North American ice dancers.

While world championships leading into the Vancouver Games will continue to be marked by change and startling results, there are some characteristics that remain virtually timeless.

Technical advances, which have driven the sport's popularity since the early 1980s, went slightly dormant in the men's division for the first couple of years of the new scoring system, and for much longer among the women. But there were 15 quads attempted by the men at the 2007 Worlds — it was impossible to win a medal without one and Tomas Verner of the Czech Republic cleanly landed two, rocketing him from ninth to fourth. The women, led by Asada, Ando, Kim, Meissner and a few others, are back at the triple Axel and nibbling around the edges of a quad explosion.

There will of course be the annual battles within the battles, noticed only by individual national federations as their skaters who finish out of the medals vie to place high enough to qualify more, or just as many, competitors for the next Worlds. Joannie Rochette, for example, staged a marvelous rally with a fifth-place freeskate in 2007 to move from 16th in the short program to 10th overall, just enough to keep Canadian content at two women.

There are always some skaters who overcome injuries and health problems to provide stirring stories at Worlds. Among those are Qing Pang and Jian Tong, who recovered from her kidney problems and his car accident to claim the 2007 pairs silver medal.

Just as common, though, are those who are unfortunately taken down by injuries at the worst time. Former world champions Maria Petrova and Alexei Tikhonov, talked out of retiring by a Russian federation worried about depth, were forced to withdraw because he injured his leg during practice for the 2007 freeskate. And popular Poles Dorota Siudek and Mariusz Siudek pulled out of the last freeskate of their careers when he re-injured his back during the warmup, forcing them to miss their farewell performance.

Disappointments like those produce tears of a different sort than in the Kiss 'n' Cry, where the most successful skaters of the final week of the season are releasing a dam of pent-up hopes, fears, frustrations and physical exhaustion from a long and hilly season.

And they all know the same thing — that almost the very next day, the next season begins.

Miki Ando/Nikolai Morozov

23

Joannie Rochette

The New Year Starts in Autumn: Grand Prix Events

Right after the Worlds, and often before, skaters begin to think about programs and music for the next season. Coaches and choreographers have already been thinking about them for some time.

During the late spring and summer, skaters also look ahead to what they'll need technically for the following season. As the international community speeds toward Vancouver 2010, it's obvious that elite men will need quads, perhaps two or three, by the next Olympics. Women will require various triple-triple combinations and perhaps a triple Axel or a quad to win. And pairs must do at least triple twists and perhaps throw triple Axels or throw quads. So even those who aren't inserting these combinations and quads into their competitive programs are trying them out in practice, hoping to master them.

Spaced throughout the income-generating spring and summer tours and exhibitions, skaters are working hard doing their fiercest practicing: blocking out programs and repeating jump after jump, spin after spin, footwork sequence after footwork sequence.

When late autumn arrives, they're ready (or should be) to show off to the world, and hopefully make a little money, too.

The Grand Prix series, for elite skaters, runs from late October to December and consists of six coordinated major events run by the International Skating Union (ISU): Skate America; Skate Canada; Cup of China; Trophée Eric Bompard in France; Cup of Russia; and the NHK Trophy in Japan.

The ISU assigns, by draw, two Grand Prix events to the top dozen skaters from the previous year, and guarantees at least one event to those in the top 24. There is a seeding system to fill out the rest of the fields, and because the age limit is 14, not 16 as at Worlds, future stars are often showcased. The specific events are assigned by the International Skating Union. If there are any extra berths, organizers of individual events may invite skaters

Top to bottom: Joannie Rochette, Fumie Suguri, Evan Lysacek

Kimmie Meissner

Born: October 4, 1989

Hometown: Towson, Maryland

Training site: Newark, Delaware

Coach: Pam Gregory

Choreographers: Nikolai Morozov; Lori Nichol

- World champion, 2006
- In 2006–07: won first U.S. Nationals; 4th, Worlds; 2nd, Skate America; 3rd, Trophée Eric Bompard; 1st, Four Continents
- 6th at 2006 Olympics
- At 16, seventh-youngest women's world champion in history
- At her first senior Nationals in 2005 — landed first triple Axel by an American woman in 14 years
- Major supporter of children's cancer programs

into a formal tour in 1995, skaters used the fall season to test out their programs in front of international judges, to gauge the competition and to gain competitive experience. Those are still strong motivations, but so is the money. Modern skaters, who came up through a similar Grand Prix system as juniors, are much tougher competitors than the generations before them. That's because they've endured many more tournaments.

The Grand Prix series is also the public's first view of the new season: who's hurt, who's hot and who's taken the necessary steps to upgrade weak points in their skating arsenal — so important in the new era of all-round skating.

Plus: who's in, and who's not.

In the fall of 2006, the skating public was informed that American superstars Michelle Kwan and Sasha Cohen were skipping the entire competitive season, and perhaps more than that, although both left the door open to return for the 2009–10 Olympic season. Kwan wanted to concentrate on college studies and make worldwide goodwill visits in her new role as the United States' first Public Diplomacy Envoy. Cohen, an aspiring actress, was trying her hand in film.

That left American women's skating wide-open, and it was appropriate that the first stop on the Grand Prix tour was Skate America, held for the first time in Hartford, Connecticut.

Skate America

In a strong indication of what was to come, later in the year and all the way to the 2010 Olympics, a horde of Japanese TV networks and print reporters were at Skate America to record every thought and deed of Miki Ando and the Asada sisters, 16-year-old Mao and 18-year-old Mai, plus 19-year-old men's contender Nobunari Oda.

With the attention around the Japanese, Kimmie Meissner was almost overshadowed as she began a season in which she hoped to defend the world championship she had won at Calgary in March,

of their choice, but no skater may compete in more than three Grand Prix events per autumn, and only the two ISU-asssigned events count for points.

There is a total purse of $180,000 for each Grand Prix event (winners receive $18,000 each), and $272,000 for the Final ($25,000 to the winners) — so a good fall season can be quite lucrative.

Before the six-country invitationals were united

and also win her first national title. In 2005, she'd landed a triple Axel at Nationals to finish third in her first year senior and hoped to have the elusive big jump under control again for later in the season. She had two big combinations ready for Hartford: a triple Lutz–triple loop and a triple flip–triple toe.

She landed the former and doubled the back end of the latter. Kimmie finished second, her best finish to date in a Grand Prix event.

Mao Asada was close to perfection in the short program, establishing a personal best in points, and was already being touted as the early favorite

Sasha Cohen

for gold at the 2010 Olympics. She faded, though, after missing her triple Axel in the long program and finished third.

The Asada sisters are such celebrities in Japan that they find it hard to relax, especially in the overcrowded training rinks where practice time is limited. So in the summer of 2006 their mother brought them to Lake Arrowhead, California. Their mom is a former gymnast who originally wanted her daughters to be ballerinas. When Mao was just three, the girls started skating, primarily to strengthen their ankles for dancing. To this day,

28

their early classical dance training is evident in both sisters' graceful limb movements and their elegant carriage. In Arrowhead, they work with coach Rafael Aratunian, who also mentors Michelle Kwan and Jeffrey Buttle. The sisters have English tutors, study Russian and get all the ice time they want.

While Mai had success on the junior Grand Prix circuit and is making some inroads internationally, Mao has the greater talent. She is a natural, light jumper who makes even the hardest tricks seem effortless. At 14, she landed her first triple Axel. Even bigger jumps are on the horizon. Arutunian raves about his new students' incredible work ethic and commitment to detail. That's a common, awe-inspired observation from coaches working with Asian skaters for the first time, and a springboard to understanding the far-eastern nations' phenomenal rise to world skating prominence.

Mai Asada finished sixth at Skate America and Mao third. But it was the other Japanese woman, Miki Ando, who started the season off on exactly the right foot, after ending the previous year on the wrong one.

Ando had placed only sixth at the talent rich Japanese Nationals in 2006, partly because of injuries that nagged her all season, yet she was named to the Olympic team. At Torino she finished a lowly 15th and didn't look good doing it. At the Worlds in Calgary a month later, Ando wasn't even on the Japanese team, having been dropped in favor of Yukari Nakano and Yoshie Onda.

Ando was a jumper who was not jumping well. Faced with severe criticism and increasing competition at home, she decided to do something about it. She came to Simsbury, Connecticut, to train under famed Nikolai Morozov, who said she just wasn't ready to compete. She worked painstakingly with Morozov, who had sculpted Shizuka Arakawa into the 2006 Olympic champion, while also spending time in Japan with coach Yuko Monna.

Ando arrived at Skate America a more prepared skater. Her jumps were crisp and her choreography,

Mao Asada

always a lesser asset, was more mature and flowing. She won easily, beating Kimmie Meissner by 15 points and launching her new season with a huge boost of confidence.

Nobunari Oda is another young Japanese skater who will face a stiff domestic battle right into the

Vancouver Games. He trains in Barrie, Ontario, with Lee Barkell, for half the year. The other half is spent in Japan with his primary coach, his mother Noriko. Oda came into the new season off a fourth-place finish at the 2006 Worlds, after losing an Olympic berth to Daisuke Takahashi.

A passionate, pensive and sometimes comedic skater, who is still working on quad consistency, Oda got his own season off to a great start with a victory with the second-highest points total ever in the short program at Skate America. He took the gold over the United States' two-time world medalist Evan Lysacek and rising French artist Alban Préaubert. Lysacek, though, won the freeskate, which is his forte.

Injuries and illness are always factors at any time in the skating season. They showed up early in 2006–07, with world champion pair Qing Pang and Jian Tong withdrawing from Skate America because of her severe kidney inflammation. Americans Rena Inoue, with a sprained foot, and John Baldwin, with a groin injury, were hurting too, but they rode adrenalin to their first victory in a Grand Prix event, winning Skate America. Like many veterans facing another four-year haul to an Olympics, Inoue and Baldwin had considered retiring, but were glad they came back. In the first event of the year, Baldwin said out loud what many other pairs teams were only thinking: "Our goal is not to let the Chinese dominate the Worlds podium."

The Polish husband-and-wife team of Darota and Mariusz Zuidek opened their retirement season with a silver medal in their first Skate America appearance in 16 years together. American pair Naomi Nari Nam and Themistocles (Themi) Leftheris, who teamed up 14 years after the Polish

Naomi Nari Nam/Themistocles Leftheris

USA

Melissa Gregory and Denis Petukhov

ICE DANCING

Born: May 22, 1981;
October 6, 1978.

Hometowns: Chicago, Illinois;
Kirov, Russia

Training site: Newark, Delaware

Coaches: Natalia Linichuk;
Gennadi Karpanosov

Choreographer: Patti Wilcox

• Melissa and Denis were
10th at 2007 Worlds, down
one spot from 2006

• In 2006–07: 2nd,
Skate America; 3rd, NHK;
6th, Grand Prix Final;
won fourth silver
at Nationals

• Looking for new
partners in 2000,
they found each
other on
the Internet

• Were married in
February 2001; he became
a U.S. citizen in February 2005

🇨🇭 SUI

Stéphane Lambiel

Born: April 2, 1985

Hometown: Saxon, Switzerland

Training site: Geneva, Switzerland

Coach: Peter Grütter

Choreographers: Salme Guadarrama;
Antonio Najarro

- Won Worlds in 2005 and '06, the first Swiss men's champ since 1947
- Won Grand Prix 2006 and Skate Canada 2006, 2nd at 2006 Olympics
- Felt he had lost competitive urge, he skipped '07 Europeans but rallied to win bronze at Worlds
- Has great ability to rise to the occasion — like Alexei Yagudin, whom he admires
- Nicknamed the Little Zebra

Gregory and Denis Petukhov, who had left Simsbury. Changing coaches and locales is common, and ice dancers often do it at the start of an Olympiad, seeking a new edge for the next four years in the most political of skating's four divisions. The top dancers are centered in only a handful of sites — Simsbury, Newark, the Detroit area and Lyon, France, among them — so it's not unusual to see a podium loaded with training partners. At Hartford in 2006, Denkova-Staviski took the gold, and Gregory-Petukhov the silver.

Skate Canada

Skate Canada, the second oldest major fall event (one year younger than the Cup of Russia), is always one week after Skate America, and some of the field is often duplicated. But in 2006, the two internationals were held on opposite coasts: Skate America in Hartford, Connecticut; and Victoria, British Columbia, playing host to Skate Canada.

Among the sport's biggest names, only Inoue-Baldwin made the transcontinental trip in the 2006–07 season. They added a silver to the previous weekend's gold. Their trademark throw triple Axel helped them barely edge (by 0.13 points) the bronze medalists, Canada's Valerie Marcoux and Craig Buntin. (A few months later, Valerie would retire. Craig still plans on skating.)

Although Olympic silver medalists Dan Zhang and Hao Zhang had trained very little because of the knee injury she suffered in a horrific fall in their Torino freeskate, the Chinese stars won Skate Canada easily.

The men's field featured two themes that should recur many times leading into the 2010 Games: lots of depth, and lots of movement between the short and long programs. Two-time world champion Stéphane Lambiel won the gold, despite finishing seventh in the short program. Daisuke Takahashi indicated that he'd be a medal contender in the new Olympiad, finishing second. American Johnny Weir won the bronze. Tomas Verner of the Czech

team first did, hinted at a bright future with a bronze in their first Grand Prix event.

Retirement thoughts are never far from the surface with older skating teams. World ice dance champions Albena Denkova and Maxim Staviski (2006) were talked out of leaving eligible ranks by the pleas of their fans in Bulgaria. So they returned to train in Newark, Delaware, where their new clubmates were American husband-and-wife Melissa

Federica Faiella/Massimo Scali

Fumie Suguri

Republic had a personal best in the short program, but settled for fourth overall.

What held Canadian fans' attention, though, were the dance and women's events. Korean teenage sensation Yu-Na Kim had taken lessons from Canadian icon Brian Orser in Toronto during the summer and was about to ask him to take over as her full-time coach. She made her senior debut by winning the short and finishing third overall, falling on a triple Lutz in the freeskate. Veteran

Fumie Suguri, coming off a world silver medal but almost forgotten on the crowded Japanese scene, showed she could not be counted out, and took silver. But it was native daughter Joannie Rochette who took gold with a dynamic freeskate, rocketing from a fifth-place short program. She admitted to nervousness but kept telling herself that "every time I have a chance to perform at home it's an opportunity to prepare for the 2010 Olympics."

Marie-France Dubreuil and Patrice Lauzon train in Lyon, France, but led a North American assault on the former European preserve of ice dancing. No North American dancers had ever won the world championship until Canadians Shae-Lynn Bourne and Victor Kraatz prevailed in 2003, and the new scoring system has helped eliminate much of the inside clout European teams had always enjoyed. After a terrible fall ended their Olympic dreams, the Canadians had come agonizingly close to winning the 2006 world championship and entered the new season fired up. Their elegantly choreographed and technically challenging freeskating is a stylistic contrast to the hyper-drama of many European teams. They are expected to vie with, among others, American rivals Tanith Belbin and Ben Agosto all the way to 2010. Dubreuil and Lauzon cruised to victory at Skate Canada, well clear of surprise runners-up Tessa Virtue and Scott Moir, the world junior champions who were in their first senior international. Italians Federica Faiella and Massimo Scali were third, and Americans Meryl Davis and Charlie White burst onto the scene with a fourth-place finish in their first Grand Prix.

Cup of China

Grand Prix competitions map the geography of national figure skating interest. A quarter-century ago, the major fall season included prestigious events in England, Holland, Austria and then-Czechoslovakia. These events have been downgraded or don't exist at all. And until 2002, one of the premier Grand Prix events was held in Germany. But the Bofrost Cup was dropped, and in 2003 the Cup of China entered the calendar to replace it. With Japan's NHK Trophy, that gives Asia one-third of the Grand Prix schedule, a barometer of not just skating depth but financial clout.

Cup of China, the third event on the circuit, usually draws heavily from Russia and Japan and, of course, is consistently deep in pairs.

In 2006 the surprise women's winner was Julia Sebestyen, the wildly inconsistent six-time Hungarian champion who has won the European title and finished in the world's top 10 three times, but has also fallen as low as 22nd in the world, as she did in Calgary just eight months earlier. Sebestyen rallied from third in the short to win the freeskate and the gold medal — narrowly beating Japan's

Tessa Virtue and Scott Moir

ICE DANCING

Born: May 17, 1989; September 2, 1987

Hometowns: London, Ontario; Ilderton,Ontario

Training site: Canton, Michigan

Coaches: Igor Shpilband; Marina Zueva

Choreographer: Igor Shpilband

- Made an incredible Worlds debut in 2007, finishing 6th

- After winning silver in 2005, became first Canadians ever to win world junior ice dance title (2006)

- Superb first senior season (2006–07): 2nd, Skate Canada, 4th, Trophée Eric Bompard; 2nd, Nationals; 3rd, Four Continents

- Scott's aunt Carol, a coach, teamed them up when Tessa was 8 and Scott 10

Julia Sebestyen

Born: May 14, 1981

Hometown: Budapest, Hungary

Training site: Budapest

Coach: Gurgen Vardanjan

Choreographer: Nina Petrenko

- Was first-ever European women's champion from Hungary (2004)

- In 2006–07: 1st, Cup of China; 2nd, Cup of Russia; 6th, Grand Prix Final; 9th, Europeans; 12th, Worlds

- Trained on an open-air rink for nine years until she was 13

graceful Yukari Nakano who, in 2002, had landed the first triple Axel by a woman in a full decade.

American Emily Hughes who, like her older sister, Olympic champion Sarah, is trying to lead a balanced life of school, social activities and high-level skating, stood first after the short program. Unfamiliar with that position, she downgraded a number of jumps in the freeskate, but still finished third, just 0.15 points from the silver, and won the first Grand Prix medal of her career.

Hughes' teammate Evan Lysacek won his first Grand Prix event, guaranteeing himself a spot in the Grand Prix Final. His competitive urge, strong spins and compelling interpretations ensure that he'll be a podium contender for 2010, as long as his newly mastered quad stays consistent. A distant second was Belarus' Sergei Davydov, who has shown a renewed commitment to training, which many observers feel could not be said of bronze medalist Emanuel Sandhu. The enigmatic and talent-blessed Canadian, who won the 2004 Grand Prix Final, is trying to establish a singing career, which may have divided his attentions. He also had difficult travel arrangements to reach China, but those are common in a fall season that spans three continents and should not affect a top performer too much.

Lysacek, meanwhile, was wrestling with a question that besets a number of skaters during the fall season: should he change his successful, but older, *Carmen* freeskate to something fresher for the new year?

"It's hard to weigh the risks of getting a new program when this is going so well," he pondered, on U.S. Figure Skating's web site. "This is a good confidence boost for me for the rest of the season."

Favorites Tanith Belbin and Ben Agosto, meanwhile, were asking the same question from a different angle after they lost the Cup of China freedance, normally their strong point. They were edged for the gold by rising Russians Oksana Domnina and Maxim Shabalin, whom they normally beat. On one hand, that verified the democracy of the new scoring system. On the other, it left the Americans wondering if their freedance to "That's Entertainment" was solid enough.

Skating before home audiences, Xue Shen and Hongbo Zhao demonstrated that they are without peers, winning the pairs competition by 21 points over Qing Pang and Jian Tong. The previous year, Shen and Zhao longingly watched Cup of China from the sidelines because of injury, and he was still suffering from Achilles tendon problems. But now their performance was elegant and the massive

RUS

Oksana Domnina and Maxim Shabalin

ICE DANCING

Born: August 17, 1984;
January 25, 1982

Hometowns: Samara, Russia;
Kirov, Russia

Training site: Odintsovo, Russia

Coach: Alexei Gorshkov

Choreographer: Sergei
Petukhov

- Capped a break-
  through season with
  a 5th-place finish at
  2007 Worlds

- In 2006–07: 1st,
  Cup of China; 2nd, Cup
  of Russia; 3rd, Grand Prix
  Final; 2nd, Europeans; won second
  national title

- Won 2003 Junior Worlds, one
  year after they teamed up

- Oksana's extreme hair
  braid became a fad
  among ice dancers in
  2006–07

Brian Joubert

Born: September 20, 1984

Hometown: Poitiers, France

Training site: Poitiers

Coach: Jean-Christophe Simond

Choreographer: Kurt Browning

- In 2007, became the first Frenchman to win world title in 42 years

- First Frenchman to win European title in 40 years (2004)

- 2006–07 his finest season: winning Trophée Eric Bompard, Cup of Russia, Grand Prix Final

- Switched coaches in summer '06 to former European medalist Jean-Christophe Simond

- Wanted to play ice hockey, but at 4 joined older sisters at skating class

throw triple loop recieved one plus-3 Grade of Execution (GOE) mark, and nine plus-2s. Such high GOEs are rare in pairs, but then Shen and Zhao are a rare pair.

Trophée Eric Bompard

After Cup of China, the ISU caravan shifts its tent to France for the Trophée Eric Bompard, known until 2003 as the Trophée de France or Trophée Lalique. It is the only major fall event remaining in western Europe, signifying two trends: the decline of interest in former European powerhouse nations, and France's sensational rise as a political, financial and competitive player.

But no male singles from the home country had ever won the event, and Brian Joubert, twice silver medalist, was determined to break that drought in mid-November 2006. He was good on his word.

With choreography provided by four-time world champion Kurt Browning, Joubert was hoping to become more consistent as he bore down on the 2010 Games.

"I've tried to change, to learn to move my whole body," he said of Browning's choreographic contribution. "That's why I went to work with him. I am confident and relaxed, and I was not like that during the Olympic season."

Joubert hit three quads over his two programs, easily beating friend, compatriot and rising star Alban Préaubert, who won silver. The two train together during the summer at Courchevel, and try to prod each other on. Joubert, the superior jumper, sets the technical bar. Préaubert, cut from cloth similar to earlier French entertainers such as Philippe Candeloro and Laurent Tobel, stimulates a greater artistic awareness in Joubert.

"There is no competition between us," Préaubert says. "I will try to help him and he does the same thing with me. It is not like a fight."

Yu-Na Kim made history in the women's division, becoming the first skater from South Korea to win a Grand Prix gold. She soars with the eagles

Alban Préaubert

Born: September, 20, 1985

Hometown: Every, France

Training site: Champigny, France

Coach: Annick Dumont

Choreographer: Nikolai Morozov

- In 2006–07: 2nd, Trophée Eric Bompard; 3rd, Skate America; 4th, Grand Prix Final; 6th, Europeans; 11th, Worlds

- Entertains in the French tradition of skaters Philippe Candeloro, Laurent Tobel and Stanick Jeannette

- Is studying for master's degree in management at a top French business school

on her jumps, but often hurts her scores with a fall, and Trophée Eric Bompard was no exception as she tumbled on her late-program double Axel. Still, she had enough to beat runner Miki Ando, who was a solid second, and Kimmie Meissner, who fell on her triple Axel attempt but was glad she had made the bid. Canada's Joannie Rochette dropped from third after the short program and finished fourth.

Russian veterans Maria Petrova and Alexei Tikhonov, former world pairs champions, won the 35th Grand Prix medal of their long careers in their

Sarah Meier

Born: May 4, 1984

Hometown: Bülach, Switzerland

Training site: Bülach, Switzerland; Oberstdorf, Germany

Coaches: Eva Fehr; Mark Pepperday

Choreographers: Salome Guadarrama; Tatiana Druchinina

- Sarah's silver in 2007 was first women's medal for Switzerland at Europeans since 1981

- In 2006–07: 1st, Cup of Russia; 4th, Skate America; 3rd, Grand Prix Final; 7th, Worlds

- Coached by her aunt Eva Fehr; her mother and sister are on same synchro team

first competition after being lured out of retirement by the worried Russian Federation. Americans Rena Inoue and John Baldwin finished second, despite a couple of falls, but since he had been diagnosed with a case of shingles the night before the short program, they considered themselves fortunate that they could compete at all.

Reigning world ice dance champions Albena Denkova and Maxim Staviski won their second Grand Prix gold in as many 2006 attempts, and qualified for the final with ease. But French champions Isabelle Delobel and Olivier Schoenfelder were only 0.06 behind the Bulgarians in the freedance, finished second and earned a surge of self-belief for the rest of the season.

Cup of Russia

In week five, the Grand Prix series moves to Russia for the Cup of Russia, which was born in 1972, making it the oldest of the major fall internationals.

Like golfers who have the odd courses that bamboozle them, skaters often carry worrisome memories of certain cities, and Moscow was a thorn in Brian Joubert's memory. He had a terrible freeskate and lost all chances of a title, plunging to sixth at the 2005 Moscow Worlds. In late 2006, he was hoping to clear that mental roadblock. He landed three quads in the freeskate — quad toe, quad toe in combination, quad Salchow — and won the Cup of Russia by 41 points over American Johnny Weir. Memory bank cleansed, his momentum continued.

The women's event, meanwhile, was unexpectedly won by Sarah Meier, a lyrical skater who captured Switzerland's first-ever women's Grand Prix gold. Hungary's Julia Sebestyen showed her inconsistent side by winning the short program and finishing fifth in the freeskate, but still took the silver medal, qualifying for the Grand Prix Final just a few months after a disastrous 2006 Olympics and Worlds.

Meanwhile, a couple of other autumn trends

continued. The once-powerful Russian women could place no higher than veteran Elena Sokolova's fourth place. And Tanith Belbin and Ben Agosto won the ice dance title, somewhat avenging their earlier loss to Oksana Domnina and Maxim Shabalin, but were once again defeated by the Russians in the freedance. If the purpose of the autumn season is partly to assess the strength of the programs, the American stars had some deep thinking to do.

Veteran competitors Maria Petrova and Alexei Tikhonov, their pictures on promotional posters for the first time, finished second in pairs, winning the

Rena Inoue/John Baldwin

RUS

Yuko Kawaguchi and Alexander Smirnov

PAIRS

Born: October 11, 1984; November 20, 1981

Hometown: Aichi, Japan; St. Petersburg, Russia;

Training site: St. Petersburg

Coach: Tamara Moskvina

Choreographer: Nikolai Velikov

- In 2006–07: 4th after short program at 2007 Worlds, 9th, overall; 3rd, Cup of Russia

- She is first foreigner to skate for Russia at a major international

- Pair missed 2007 Europeans and Russian Nationals when she broke her ankle

- Originally a singles skater, Yuko teamed up with Alexander Markuntsov (of Russia) to win Japan's first-ever ISU pairs medal (silver, 2001, Junior Worlds)

freeskate. Germany's Aliona Savchenko and Robin Szolkowy edged them for the gold but the real story, and a disturbing one for Russian skating, was the bronze medal.

Yuko Kawaguchi, from Aichi, Japan, became the first non-Russian to skate for the country at a major competition in the century-plus history of the sport. She and her partner, Alexander Smirnov of St. Petersburg, finished third in Moscow and eventually qualified for the Worlds, where they were the highest-ranked Russians. The irony is that in tandem events (pairs and dance), Russia has traditionally been the exporter, not the importer, of talent.

Kawaguchi has broken international ground before. She skated singles for Japan and wanted to skate for Tamara Moskvina, but the legendary coach said she coached only pairs. So Kawaguchi came to the United States and skated with Russian Alexander Markuntsov. Together they represented Japan and won the silver medal at the 2001 world junior championship.

That was the first international medal ever won by a pairs skater from Japan. When Moskvina moved home to St. Petersburg, Kawaguchi followed and was paired with Smirnov in 2006. If they continue to rise, she may petition Japan for the rare privilege of dual citizenship so she can represent Russia in the 2010 Games.

NHK Trophy

The NHK Trophy in Japan wraps up the fall international competitions and is the last chance for skaters to mount the points needed to qualify for the Grand Prix Final.

As expected, given weak entries from most other countries, Japan swept the podium at Nagano in both singles events. Daisuke Takahashi, Nobunari Oda and world junior champion Takahiko Kozuka finished 1-2-3 in men's. Mao Asada, Fumie Suguri and Yukari Nakano repeated the feat in women's. Asada stepped out of the triple Axel landing, but her total score of 199.52 was the highest ever by a woman.

Canada's Marie-France Dubreuil and Patrice Lauzon unveiled a new original dance and romped to the gold medal, well ahead of Jana Khokhlova and Sergei Novitski. But the Russian silver medalists surprised U.S. couple Melissa Gregory and Denis

GER

Aliona Savchenko and Robin Szolkowy

PAIRS

Born: January 19, 1984; July 14, 1979

Hometown: Kiev, Ukraine; Greifswald, Germany

Training site: Chemnitz, Germany

Coach: Ingo Steuer

Choreographer: Ingo Steuer

• Are restoring the luster of German pairs skating with their 2007 European championship and Worlds bronze medal

• Also in 2006–07: 1st, Cup of Russia; 3rd, Cup of China; 2nd, Grand Prix Final

• She received her German citizenship in January, 2006, so the pair could skate at the Olympics (6th)

• She won 2000 Junior Worlds for Ukraine with Stanislav Morozov

Johnny Weir

Born: July 2, 1984

Hometown: Coatesville, Pennsylvania

Training site: Newark, Delaware; Simsbury, Connecticut

Coaches: Priscilla Hill; Marina Anissina

Choreographer: Marina Anissina

- Was 8th at 2007 Worlds after finishing as high as 4th (2005)

- In 2006–07: 2nd, Cup of Russia; 3rd, Skate Canada; 3rd, Nationals

- U.S. champion, 2004, 2005, 2006; won world junior title in 2001

- Inspiration to skate was watching Oksana Baiul win 1994 Olympics

Petukhov, who took the bronze medal in the often unpredictable discipline.

Xue Shen and Hongbo Zhao, despite Xue's injured ankle, easily won the pairs event over Dan Zhang and Hao Zhang and were a full 27 points ahead of third place Canadians Valerie Marcoux and Craig Buntin.

After the NHK, for those who don't qualify for the Grand Prix Final, it's back home for Nationals. For those elite six per division who do qualify, it's a short two weeks until they must peak for what is, in effect, a midseason world championship.

Grand Prix Final

Although most skaters take part in only two Grand Prix competitions, they're usually tightly spaced and involve intercontinental travel. The fall season can therefore take its toll. By the time the Grand Prix Final rolls around, injuries and illnesses begin to mount. Often, alternates who have just failed to make the top six in the Grand Prix point standings find themselves in the prestigious final, because injury or fatigue has forced a qualifier to skip the event.

In 2004, for example, Canada's Emanuel Sandhu was a late substitute and won the Grand Prix Final in the middle of his finest season. In 2006, Ben Agosto hurt his back practicing a lift and he and Tanith Belbin were forced to withdraw. It was fortunate that promising Russians Jana Khokhlova and Sergei Novitski were the alternates, because they live in Moscow and the Grand Prix Final was not far away, in the famous Ice Palace of St. Petersburg. And although there were reports that Alban Préaubert, a surprise qualifier, would be forced out by injury, he managed to make it to St. Petersburg.

By the middle of the second day of the 2006 event, one-third of the men's field had withdrawn. Evan Lysacek injured his hip on a fall in the opening practice, and his American teammate Johnny Weir pulled out during the next morning's practice, also with an injured hip. Daisuke Takahashi was ill

USA

Evan Lysacek

Born: June 4, 1985

Hometown: Chicago, Illinois

Training site: El Segundo, California

Coach: Frank Carroll

Choreographers: Lori Nichol; Kurt Browning

- Slipped to 5th at 2007 Worlds, after two straight bronze medals

- 2006–07, though, was most consistent season: won first national title; 1st, Cup of China; 2nd, Skate America; 1st, Four Continents

- Has won U.S. juvenile, novice, junior and senior titles; was 4th at 2006 Olympics

- Very strong competitive drive — landed quad to win Nationals; near-clean quad combination to overcome 11-point deficit at 2007 Four Continents

but decided to skate because the field was already so depleted, and hung in to win the silver medal, beating his national rival Nobunari Oda, who was third. Brian Joubert completed a brilliant fall season with the gold medal, although he didn't skate as well as he had in his earlier events.

The women faced another kind of problem:

Yu-Na Kim

Sarah Meier, Fumie Suguri and Julia Sebestyen were all stuck in a traffic jam, delaying the start of the short program by 20 minutes. It was no coincidence that, shaken, they occupied the bottom three spots in the short, while Mao Asada, Miki Ando and Yu-Na Kim finished 1-2-3 in the short. But Sarah Meier rallied in the freeskate, despite downgrading some jumps, riding her tremendous spins (a longtime Swiss tradition) to the bronze medal. Asada struggled, falling on her triple Axel, to drop to the silver medal. Kim, skating with a back injury that would plague her all season, moved from third to first.

Albena Denkova and Maxim Staviski wrapped up the first half of their farewell season with another victory in the dance, after Canadian leaders Marie-France Dubreuil and Patrice Lauzon had a stumble and barely held off Oksana Domnina and Maxim Shabalin for third.

In pairs, Xue Shen and Hongbo Zhao cruised to victory in their perfect season. Aliona Savchenko was battling injury, but she and Robin Szolkowy finished second, as Dan Zhang and Hao Zhang faded because she fell very ill and was taken to a hospital after the freeskate. She was later diagnosed with deficiencies of calcium and potassium.

The most frightening injury of the event, though, occurred after it was over. American pairs skater John Baldwin, who had finished fourth with Rena Inoue, was at a nightclub near his hotel when he was mugged by unknown assailants, robbed and left unconscious. He suffered vertigo for three weeks afterward, but recovered sufficiently in time for U.S. Nationals. The terrifying assault left its emotional scars but Baldwin said, "when I'm skating I don't think about it. Skating has helped me a lot with that."

Dan Zhang
and Hao Zhang

PAIRS

Born: October 4, 1985; July 6, 1984

Hometown: Harbin, China

Training site: Beijing, China

Coach: Yao Ming

Choreographer: Gorsha Sur

• Were 2nd at 2006 Olympics and Worlds, despite her sprained ligaments after a horrible fall on an attempted throw quadruple Salchow

• In 2006–07:1st, Skate Canada; 2nd, NHK; 3rd, Grand Prix Final; 5th, Worlds

• Junior world champions, 2001

• Landed first quad throw ever in history of Junior Worlds (2000)

• They are not related

Kimmie Meissner

Home for the Holidays ...
and the National Championships

Once the Grand Prix season is over, skaters usually return to their own countries for the period straddling New Year's to compete in their national championship, which normally doubles as the qualifying event for the world team.

For many, who are among only one or two elite skaters in their countries, the Nationals are little more than a formality. But for others, because of the depth of talent at home, the national championships are nearly as important as any other competition on the yearly calendar, including the Worlds.

American women of the early 1990s, for instance, used to say that the world championships weren't as pressure-packed as U.S. Nationals, because the audiences were often smaller and there were sometimes fewer skaters who could beat you. Kristi Yamaguchi and Kimmie Meissner, for example, won world titles before they won their U.S. titles, and 2002 Olympic champion Sarah

Hughes never was champion of the United States. Until recently, Russia had similarly spectacular depth in pairs and dance.

Japanese Nationals

The same ultracompetitive situation now exists in Japan. In any given year, at least five Japanese women could reasonably expect to finish on or near the podium at Worlds — provided they make it out of their own Nationals, with a maximum of three berths available.

For the 2007 Worlds, the Japanese team included young sensation Mao Asada, who won her first national title in the last week of December, aided by landing a triple Axel. Miki Ando, recovering from an injury-plagued sixth-place the previous year, fell on her final freeskate jump and finished second, while Yukari Nakano attempted, but fell on, a triple Axel and took bronze to earn the final world berth. That, however, meant that veterans Fumie Suguri (4th), Yoshie Onda (5th) and sixth-place Aki Sawada, who has landed

---

Top to bottom: Kimmie Meissner, Alissa Czisny, Jeffrey Buttle

49

JPN

Yukari Nakano

Born: August 25, 1985

Hometown: Tokyo, Japan

Training site: Yokohama, Japan

Coach: Nobuo Sato

Choreographer: Marina Zueva

- Was 5th at Worlds in both 2006 and 2007
- In 2006–07: 2nd, Cup of China; 3rd, NHK; 3rd, Grand Prix Final; 1st, Asian Games
- Yukari and Russia's Ludmila Nelidina each landed a triple Axel at 2002 Skate America, the first ones since Midori Ito at the 1992 Olympics

Torino. The embarrassed federation sent Oda to Worlds and he finished just off the podium in fourth, ironically earning that second berth at Worlds, which would make the 2007 Nationals less stressful for him and his rival.

Although they share several things — both won Junior Worlds, both study and skate at Kansai College (which recently built a new rink for elite skaters) and both train for long periods in North America (Takahashi in Simsbury, Connecticut; Oda in Barrie, Ontario) — they are different skaters. Oda is more consistent, is a tremendous spinner and applies a thoughtful, flowing technique to David Wilson's choreography. Takahashi is lightning in a bottle, capable of brilliant explosions of dynamic performance when he's on. He attacks his quad toe loop while Oda is still trying to master his.

The pair had the two highest point totals of the season at NHK, with Takahashi winning. And just a few weeks later, Takahashi won the 2007 Nationals with a far superior freeskate. But both men advanced to Worlds in their home country.

Canadian Nationals

In Canada and the United States, the Nationals are events *unto* themselves. Even in down years internationally, the domestic championships are held in large arenas, receive heavy media coverage and are accorded live, prime-time TV coverage. The two North American skating powers often hold their Nationals during the same week in early January.

In 2007, the Canadian Nationals were in Halifax, Nova Scotia, one of the most enthusiastic skating cities in the world, and there was the usual array of intriguing stories. Among them were the varied plights of three former champions: Emanuel Sandhu, Jeffrey Buttle and Cynthia Phaneuf.

Phaneuf was just 15 when she won the 2004 championship, but wasn't sent to Worlds. She made the Grand Prix Final the following year, but then suffered injuries and endured a tremendous growth spurt, which combined to keep her off the ice for 10

triple Axels, were left off the team. Only a few days earlier, Suguri had finished fourth in the Grand Prix Final, and the previous year, she had finished second at Worlds and fourth at the Olympics. Now that's a tough room!

And the Japanese men's division isn't much easier, although it's not as deep. At the 2006 Japanese Nationals, Nobunari Oda was announced as the winner and presented with his gold medal, but then a scoring error was discovered and Daisuke Takahashi was awarded the title, and Japan's sole berth at the Olympics. He finished only eighth at

JPN

Nobunari Oda

Born: March 25, 1987

Hometown: Takatsuki City, Japan

Training sites: Osaka, Japan;
Barrie, Ontario

Coaches: Noriko Oda; Lee Barkell

Choreographer: David Wilson

• Finished fourth at Worlds in
2006, but slipped to 7th in 2007

• In 2006–07: 1st, Skate
America; 2nd, NHK; 3rd
Grand Prix Final

• World junior champion, 2005

• Is 17th descendant of a famous
16th-century Japanese warlord

Jeffrey Buttle

Joannie Rochette

Born: January 13, 1986

Hometown: Île Dupas, Quebec

Training site: St.Leonard, Quebec

Coaches: Manon Perron; Nathalie Martin; Daniele Robillard

Choreographers: David Wilson; Sandra Bezic

- Rebounded from 16th to 10th with 5th-place freeskate at 2007 Worlds

- Won third national title in 2007

- In 2006-07: 1st, Skate Canada; 4th, Trophée Eric Bompard; 3rd, Four Continents

- Moved from 9th to 5th at 2006 Olympics with a 6-triple freeskate

- Nicknamed the Rocket, for her speed on ice

Mira Leung

Born: March 28, 1989

Hometown: Vancouver, British Columbia

Training site: Burnaby, British Columbia

Coach: Joanne McLeod

Choreographer: Joanne McLeod

- 24th at 2007 Worlds, after 13th in '06; 12th at Torino Olympics
- In 2006–07: 6th, Skate Canada; 8th, Skate America
- Following 2005–06 season, switched coaches briefly but went back to McLeod
- Won bronze at Nationals when she was 16 (2005), silver the next two years
- Skipped novice and Junior Nationals — senior debut at age 13

medal since 1973, both by Elizabeth Manley in 1988, and Rochette hopes to break that drought soon. She won her third successive title in 2007. If she runs the table to the Olympic year, she would match Jennifer Robinson's record of six national championships.

"It feels like the Olympics are coming quickly, and you have to stay ahead of your competition," said Rochette, who lacks only week-long consistency to reach the world podium.

Chasing her toward Vancouver will be Mira Leung, who came to Halifax as a more mature skater. Leung, then 17, had changed coaches briefly during the season but was back with her original mentor, Joanne McLeod, who is also Emanuel Sandhu's lifelong coach. Leung has added power and won her second successive silver medal to make the world team.

But Leung wasn't as close to Rochette as she was to third-place Lesley Hawker — the feel-good story of Canadian skating — who received a standing ovation for her second-place short program. Hawker didn't start competing until she was 15. As the oldest of 10 children, she later paid for her own lessons at Mariposa Skating Club by waiting tables for 30 to 40 hours a week. She didn't even qualify for Senior Nationals until 2002, when she was 21 — an age when some recent Olympic champions had already retired — and didn't win a medal until she took bronzes in 2006 and 2007. Unfortunately, Canada had only two world spots both those years. Hawker was always a good jumper and, with maturity, has evolved greatly in her presentation skills. She trains in Michigan and her husband works in Toronto, so the road to 2010, when she'll be 28, will be a difficult one for her. Hawker has already proven she can handle more obstacles than most skaters.

The 2007 Nationals was the first competition of the season for Olympic, Worlds and Grand Prix Final medalist Jeffrey Buttle, who had been laid up with a spinal stress fracture, initially caused by the triple Axel. Buttle is still searching for a

months and off the national scene for a year-and-a-half. She had to relearn all her jumps and returned to Nationals a mature, strong woman, finishing a respectable fourth.

In her early teens, Phaneuf went head-to-head with Joannie Rochette, but Rochette has since ascended to the world's top 10, with three Grand Prix victories and a fifth-place Olympic finish. Canada has won just one world and one Olympic

CAN

Lesley Hawker

Born: May 1, 1981

Hometown: Barrie, Ontario

Training site: Rochester Hills, Michigan

Coach: Richard Callaghan

Choreographers: Richard Callaghan; David Wilson

- In 2006–07: 3rd, Nationals; 7th, Four Continents

- Did not compete until age 15 — won first national medal at 24

- Married longtime boy-friend Jamie Doherty in June 2006

CAN

Christopher Mabee

Born: August 20, 1985

Hometown: Tillsonburg, Ontario

Training site: Barrie, Ontario

Coaches: Lee Barkell; Doug Leigh

Choreographers: David Wilson; Lori Nichol

- In 2007, won first senior national medal (silver); 13th at debut Worlds; 5th at Four Continents

- Won silver medal at 2006 Four Continents

- 3rd at 2004 Junior Grand Prix Final

- Family had backyard rink when he was young

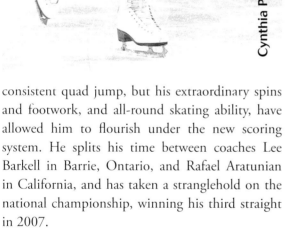

Cynthia Phaneuf

Anabelle Langlois/Cody Hay

consistent quad jump, but his extraordinary spins and footwork, and all-round skating ability, have allowed him to flourish under the new scoring system. He splits his time between coaches Lee Barkell in Barrie, Ontario, and Rafael Aratunian in California, and has taken a stranglehold on the national championship, winning his third straight in 2007.

Buttle's Mariposa training partner Christopher Mabee rode a terrific short program to his first national medal in either senior or junior, finishing second and earning a berth to Worlds. With solid jumps and improved mental toughness, he hopes

to move up the world standings approaching the Vancouver Olympics.

Emanuel Sandhu, meanwhile, continued his struggles by finishing third. Once hailed as the certain successor to the Brian Orser–Kurt Browning–Elvis Stojko championship mantle, he has been surpassed by Buttle, and Canadian skating fans are vexed by his competitive inconsistency. The audience was vocally restless after he fell on his quad and popped a triple Axel in the short program.

In Canada, which has a rich heritage in the event, pairs are taken very seriously and few national champions ever feel completely secure

CAN

Emanuel Sandhu

Born: November 18, 1980

Hometown: Richmond Hill, Ontario

Training site: Burnaby, British Columbia

Coach: Joanne McLeod

Choreographer: Joanne McLeod

- After finishing 5th at 2006 Worlds, had a difficult 2006–07 season: 3rd at Cup of China; but 3rd at Nationals (his lowest ever); 9th at Four Continents; 16th at Worlds

- Won 2004 Grand Prix Final, handing Evgeny Plushenko a rare defeat

- Two-time Skate Canada champion (2004, 2005)

- Expressive skater — started ballet at age 3, and studied 10 years at famed National Ballet School

September knee surgery. With their flow, close side-by-side elements and French-English heritage, they remind many of a young Jamie Salé and David Pelletier.

The pairs bronze went to the relatively new team of Anabelle Langlois and Cody Hay whose trademark throw triple Lutz reaps them huge technical points. As Langlois-Hay mature as a team, it should be an interesting domestic battle all the way to the Vancouver Games.

Ice dancing at Canadian Nationals is not so much a competition as a coronation. In 2006, the elegant, fast and technically precise Marie-France Dubreuil and Patrice Lauzon — a couple on and off the ice — overcame a terrifying Olympic fall to come within a whisker of winning Canada's second world ice dance championship. After teaming up in 1995, they struggled financially and had to work several jobs to support their skating careers, which seemed stalled before they moved to Lyon, France, in 2002. Under renowned coach Muriel Zazoui's innovative tutelage they moved slowly, but steadily, up the ranks until they took a huge leap from seventh to second in 2006. Unshackled by the new international judging system, which rids dance of some but not all of its previous favoritism and rigidity, Dubreuil and Lauzon now lead a North American surge in what had been the most European of all disciplines. They won their fifth national title, and fourth in a row, in 2007.

Tessa Virtue and Scott Moir, the 2006 world junior champions, continued their rapid rise by finishing second and have readjusted their sights to an Olympic medal at Vancouver. Although they are smaller and therefore must work harder to gain speed and power than most dance teams, the young couple have caught the world's attention with their difficult elements and tremendous unison.

Andrew Poje and Kaitlyn Weaver finished a surprising third at 2007 Canadians, to qualify for Worlds. They'd been united only six months earlier, and Texas-born Weaver needed a waiver from the

at Canadians. Competition-toughened Valerie Marcoux and Craig Buntin were three-time champions heading into 2007, but struggled much of the season and suffered falls in the freeskate to lose their title to rising stars Jessica Dubé and Bryce Davison. The new champions, who have survived a litany of injuries, overcame a bad fall, which injured Dubé's back during summer training, and her late-

Jessica Dubé
and Bryce Davison

PAIRS

Born: October 29,1987; January 29, 1986

Hometowns: Drummondville, Quebec;
Cambridge, Ontario

Training site: Drummondville, Quebec

Coaches: Annie Barabé; Sophie Richard;
Yvan Desjardins

Choreographers: Kevin Wheeler;
Beccy Magliarisi

• Won first Nationals January 2007;
were runners-up the previous year

• Despite season of horrible injuries, Jessica and
Bryce held onto 7th-place ranking at 2007 Worlds

• 10th in Olympics debut (2006)

• 1st, Junior Grand Prix Final; 2nd, Junior Worlds
(2004–05)

• Often compared to Olympic champions Jamie
Salé and David Pelletier in speed and unison

USA

Tanith Belbin and Ben Agosto

ICE DANCING

Born: July 11, 1984;
January 15, 1982

Hometowns: Kirkland,
Quebec; Chicago, Illinois

Training site: Canton,
Michigan

Coaches: Igor Shpilband;
Marina Zueva

Choreographer: Igor
Shpilband

- Finished 3rd at 2007
  and 2006 Worlds; 2nd
  in 2005

- 2006–07: 1st, Cup of Russia;
  2nd, Cup of China; 2nd,
  Four Continents; won fourth
  national title

- Silver at 2006 Games — first
  U.S. Olympic dance medal
  in 30 years

- World junior champions,
  2002

- Tanith, raised in Canada,
  received U.S. citizenship
  New Year's Eve 2005,
  making her eligible for
  Torino Olympics

United States Figure Skating Association to compete in Canada. In a mirror image of Tanith Belbin's career path, Weaver plans to pursue Canadian citizenship to enable her to compete at the 2010 Olympics.

U.S. Nationals

One of the purposes of the fall season is to evaluate a new program, and Tanith Belbin and Ben Agosto did just that. Their "That's Entertainment" freedance was poorly received during the 2006 fall

Evan Lysacek

61

🇺🇸 USA

Brooke Castile and Benjamin Okolski

PAIRS

Born: May 31,1986; November 12, 1984

Hometowns: Gross Pointe Woods, Michigan; Ann Arbor, Michigan

Training site: Canton, Michigan

Coach: Johnny Johns

Choreographer: Marina Zueva

- 12th in Worlds debut, 2007
- Went from 8th in 2006 Nationals to gold medal in 2007
- Won 2006 Nebelhorn Trophy at Oberstdorf, Germany

medal in 30 years. Belbin started as an ice dancer in Canada, switched to pairs to gain strength, then came back to dance in 1998, moving to Michigan to team with Agosto. Because she was Canadian, they were ineligible to compete at the 2002 Olympics, despite finishing second at Nationals. But she received her citizenship just in time for the 2006 Games. They have inspired a whole generation of Americans to take up ice dancing, and easily won their fifth straight national title in 2007.

Another international union, Melissa Gregory and Denis Petukhov, who have been married since 2001, and competed against each other at the 1998 world junior championships (he for Russia), won their fourth successive silver medal. They switched training coaches before the 2006–07 season, hoping to change their style, and were rewarded with a personal best in the freedance.

The dance bronze went to graduating juniors Meryl Davis and Charlie White, who train with Belbin and Agosto. They're part of the North American invasion hoping to crowd the podium at the 2010 Games.

There always seems to be an upset at U.S. Nationals, and in 2007 it occurred in pairs. In their first two years of senior, Brooke Castile and Ben Okolski had never been higher than eighth. But they delivered two strong programs, including a first-place freeskate, to nip three-time champions Rena Inoue and John Baldwin by 0.35 points. Castile and Okolski have brought the difficult, if under-marked, triple twist back to U.S. pairs skating, and Baldwin said they inspired him and his partner to revive theirs.

If the triple twist is the signature move of the 2007 champions, the throw triple Axel distinguishes Inoue and Baldwin from the other pairs. But, in an injury-plagued season, they were inconsistent with the huge throw and missed it at Nationals. Baldwin and Inoue are one of the most intriguing pairs in the sport. He has been on the

season, so the American champions scrubbed it and came up with theme music from *Amélie,* a French movie about an innovative woman who helps people in creative ways. As well as introducing new music and new choreography, and developing new lifts and footwork, the couple also had to regain practice time after Agosto's back injury kept them out of the Grand Prix Final.

Belbin and Agosto were coming off a silver medal at Torino, the United States' first Olympic dance

USA

Meryl Davis and Charlie White

ICE DANCING

Born: January 1, 1987;
October 24, 1987

Hometowns: West Bloomfield, Michigan;
Bloomfield Hills, Michigan

Training site: Canton, Michigan

Coaches: Igor Shpilband; Marina Zueva

Choreographers: Igor Shpilband; Marina Zueva

- Finished a strong 7th at 2007 Worlds, best U.S. dance debut in 33 years

- In 2006–07: 4th, Skate Canada; 4th, NHK; 4th, Four Continents; 3rd, U.S. Nationals

- Teamed up in 1997

- Meryl learned to skate on a lake; Charlie broke his ankle playing hockey, affecting their 2004–05 season

national team at various levels since 1986, and was the 1990 world junior bronze medalist in men's singles. Four years later his future partner finished fifth at Junior Worlds in women's singles, skating for Japan, which she also represented in pairs. She moved to the United States in 1996, and in late 1998 was diagnosed with lung cancer, the same disease that claimed her father the year before. She underwent therapy, told no one of her ordeal and was eventually cancer-free.

Naomi Nari Nam was also a very promising singles skater, and when she was just 13 finished second to Michelle Kwan in the 1999 Nationals. She was too young for the world team, but seemed

Rena Inoue and John Baldwin

PAIRS

Born: October 17, 1976; October 18, 1973;

Hometowns: Nishinomiya, Japan; Dallas, Texas

Training site: Artesia, California

Coach: Peter Oppegard

Choreographer: Peter Oppegard

- After finishing 4th in 2006, slipped to 8th at 2007 Worlds

- In 2006–07: 1st, Skate America; 2nd, Skate Canada and Trophée Eric Bompard; 4th, Grand Prix Final; 3rd, Four Continents; 2nd, Nationals

- First pair ever to land a throw triple Axel (2006 U.S. Nationals, Olympics and Worlds)

- Two-time U.S. champions

Naomi Nari Nam and Themistocles Leftheris

PAIRS

Born: July 6, 1985; December 20,1982

Hometowns: Anaheim,California; Tarpon Springs, Florida

Training site: Artestia, California

Coaches: Peter Oppegard; Karen Kwan-Oppegard

Choreographer: Peter Oppegard

- In second full season together in 2006–07, Naomi and Themi won bronze at Nationals and Skate America; were 6th at Four Continents

- She finished second to Michelle Kwan at 1999 Nationals, but hip injury in 2001 ended singles career

- He started skating at age 12, inspired by 1994 Olympics

destined for greatness as a singles skater until she incurred a serious hip injury two years later. That curtailed her singles career, so in 2005 she decided to try pairs skating with Themi Leftheris. She had no experience with pairs, and was the sixth partner for Leftheris, who had never been higher than 13th at Senior Nationals. But in just their second season together, they finished third at Skate America and won the bronze medal at Nationals, qualifying for the world championships.

Evan Lysacek has enjoyed success internationally, winning bronzes at both the 2005 and 2006 world championships and winning five Grand Prix medals, but he was unable to beat three-time U.S. champion

🇺🇸 USA

Emily Hughes

Born: January 26, 1989

Hometown: Great Neck, New York

Training site: Great Neck

Coach: Bonni Retzkin

Choreographers: David Wilson; Mark Mitchell

- 9th, Worlds (2007); 8th (2006)
- In 2006–07: 5th, Skate America; 3rd, Cup of China; 2nd, Nationals; 2nd, Four Continents
- Emily watched the 2006 Olympics opening ceremonies at home on TV, then was added to U.S. team for injured Michelle Kwan; flew to Torino and finished 7th
- Has had same coach for entire career

The premier event of the U.S. championships has always been the women's skate-off, and Kimmie Meissner grabbed the spotlight with her first national senior championship. Like Evan Lysacek, her 2007 title gave her the national triple crown: novice, junior and senior championships. Although she was only third in the freeskate, her strong short program and five triples in the freeskate were enough to give her the title. Runner-up Emily Hughes' fall on a triple flip probably cost her the national crown her older sister, Olympic champion Sarah, never wore. Like Sarah, Emily showed a fighting spirit after the fall, closing strongly.

But the big finish went to Alissa Czisny. She had appeared headed for a major breakthrough after winning 2005 Skate Canada and being the only American in the 2006 Grand Prix Final. She had been plagued by inconsistency, but she landed five triples and exhibited her terrific spins and flexibility in the freeskate at 2007 Nationals, moving from fifth to third and holding the crowd in the palm of her hand.

And what a crowd it was: a record 154,893 paid admissions, proving that although international skating has taken a huge dip in popularity on American TV, the national championship is still one of the most prestigious events in U.S. sport.

Johnny Weir at Nationals. That all changed in 2007 when Lysacek, in the midst of a tremendous season, annihilated the competition. Performing just before Weir in the freeskate, he landed a clean quad-triple combination and seven more triples including a triple Axel–triple toe. Weir tried a quad toe himself and stayed on his feet, but he two-footed and made several other errors to finish third. Ryan Bradley, who had never finished higher than eighth in six prior Nationals, rose to the occasion and topped his previous best freeskate by 38 points to capture the silver medal and his first world berth.

Ryan Bradley

USA

Alissa Czisny

Born: June 25,1987

Hometown: Sylvania, Ohio

Training site: Bloomfield Hills, Michigan

Coaches: Julianne Berlin; Elizabeth Swallow

Choreographers: David Wilson; Kurt Browning; Theresa McKendry

• In 2007, won her first national senior medal (bronze)

• In 2006–07: 4th, Skate Canada; 9th, Cup of Russia; 5th, Four Continents; 15th, Worlds

• Twin sister Amber skated singles internationally, now ice dances

Carolina Kostner

Winter: Something Old, Something New

European Championships

The European championships have a mystique that transcends the sport and are rooted in the 19th-century continent-wide explosion of skating popularity. The first world championships are now accepted as the 1896 event in St. Petersburg, Russia. Until 1924, when the United States sent a representative, no other continents were involved. And, until Barbara Ann Scott and Dick Button became dominant in 1947 and '48, North Americans were permitted to compete in the European championships partly because Americans and Canadians weren't considered a real threat.

Before the institution of the new international system of scoring, the spectacular emergence of the Asian nations and the 1999 introduction of the Four Continents, the European championships provided European skaters with unfair advantages. It was an extra–big-time competition, at a critical moment, in front of ISU judges. Alterations made to fall-season programs received important critical response before Worlds. Momentum and buzz were built up in an era when political favor was extremely important. In the darkest cases, backroom alliances were forged. Many countries, including powerhouse Russia, still use Europeans as a critical piece of evidence when choosing their world teams.

Because of the number of countries involved (still a majority of ISU member-ship), and the centuries-long association of skating with European royalty, the title "European Champion" carried a lot of weight. Even today, if a skater performs poorly at Worlds but wins Europeans, it is considered a decent season. Thus the European championships maintain a certain stateliness, perhaps second only to the Worlds, despite a diminishing importance on the actual competitive scene.

As the skating world headed toward the Vancouver Olympics, the International Skating Union awarded the 2009 Europeans to Helsinki,

Top to bottom: Carolina Kostner, Jessica Dubé, Evan Lysacek

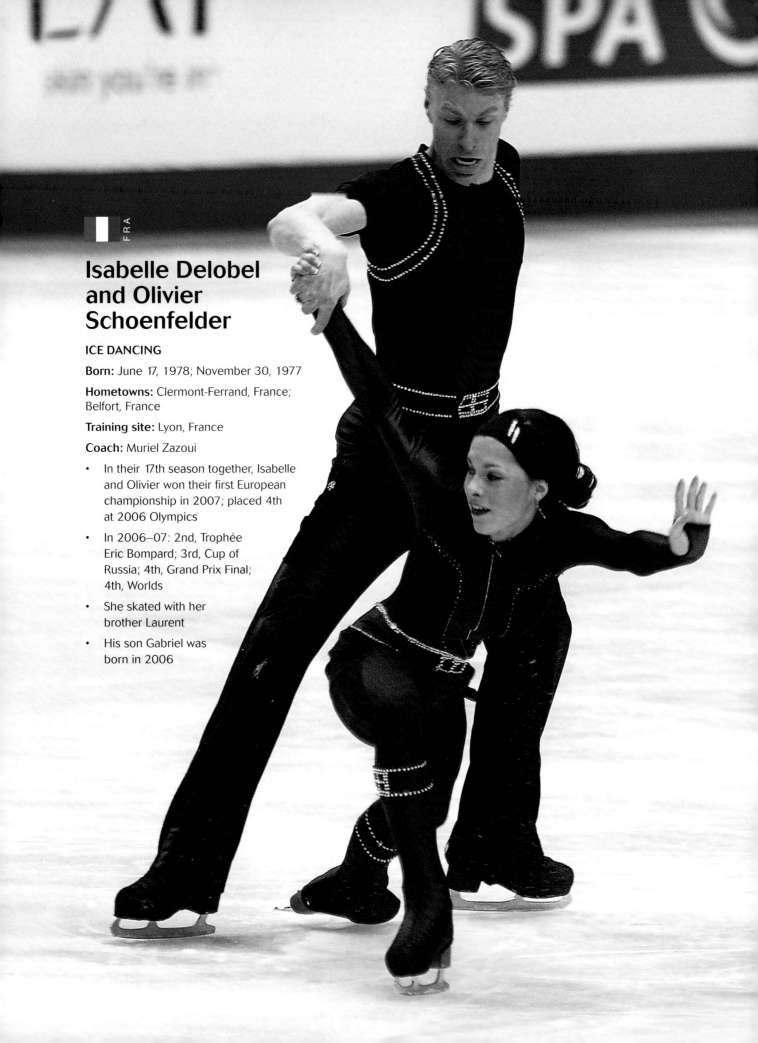

FRA

Isabelle Delobel and Olivier Schoenfelder

ICE DANCING

Born: June 17, 1978; November 30, 1977

Hometowns: Clermont-Ferrand, France; Belfort, France

Training site: Lyon, France

Coach: Muriel Zazoui

- In their 17th season together, Isabelle and Olivier won their first European championship in 2007; placed 4th at 2006 Olympics

- In 2006–07: 2nd, Trophée Eric Bompard; 3rd, Cup of Russia; 4th, Grand Prix Final; 4th, Worlds

- She skated with her brother Laurent

- His son Gabriel was born in 2006

Finland, and the 2008 event to Zagreb, Croatia. In 2007, Europeans came to Warsaw, Poland, for the first time in 99 years.

Polish icons Dorota and Mariusz Siudek arrived in Warsaw to compete at Europeans for the last time. The popular couple, who were married in May 2000 after he proposed to her during the closing banquet at Worlds, had trained in Montreal since 2003 and had gained a legion of fans in their 13 years of international skating. Their bronze in 1999 is the only world championship medal ever won by a Polish pairs team, and they wanted to leave Europe in style, before heading to the Tokyo Worlds and then into retirement.

Before a wildly appreciative crowd, and skating to carefully chosen music from iconic Polish composer Frédéric Chopin, the Siudeks won the bronze medal for a perfect sendoff.

"Our dream was to finally compete in Warsaw and win a medal at home," Mariusz Siudek said. "Tokyo will just be a good-bye to our fans."

Veteran Russians Maria Petrova and Alexei Tikhonov won the silver medal and the gold went to Aliona Savchenko and Robin Szolkowy, who unleashed booming triple throws and the now must-have triple twist. But what's most noticeable about the German pair is their blurring speed on spins. They broke an 11-year Russian stranglehold on the top of the podium to become the first pair from Germany to capture the European title since 1995, when Mandy Woetzel and Ingo Steuer won. Fittingly, Steuer is their coach. They had spent much of the season distracted by the controversy surrounding him. Accused of informing on East German athletes during the era of the Stasi secret police, Steuer was not funded by the German Olympic Committee and had to pay his own way to competitions. But the loyal Savchenko and Szolkowy refused to train with anyone else.

Although they were fourth at 2006 Worlds, and had been skating together since 1990, French dance team Isabelle Delobel and Olivier Schoenfelder

weren't given much chance of winning the 2007 European title, mainly because of the presence of reigning world champions Albena Denkova and Maxim Staviski. The Bulgarians had just won the Grand Prix Final and seemed in fine form, but the rink in Warsaw was narrower in the corners than other rinks, so they struggled with some of their patterns and could finish only third.

Dorota Siudek/
Mariusz Siudek

Aliona Savchenko/Robin Szolkowy

Delobel and Schoenfelder won the compulsory dance and original dance and finished second in the freedance to Oksana Domnina and Maxim Shabalin, holding off the Russians to win the title by a mere 0.31 points. Delobel and Schoenfelder have innovative choreography but have been inconsistent performers, and their first European title tasted even sweeter because it was so unexpected.

France took another gold when Brian Joubert continued his excellent season with the second

CZE

Tomas Verner

Born: June 3, 1986

Hometown: Borvany, Czech Republic

Training sites: Prague, Czech Republic; Oberstdorf, Germany

Coaches: Vlasta Koprivov; Michael Huth

Choreographer: Iveta Bidarova

• Made a stunning break-through in 2007 with 2nd at Europeans, 4th at Worlds

• In 2006–07: 5th, Skate Canada; 4th, Cup of Russia; won Nebelhorn Trophy at Oberstdorf, Germany

• First Czech man to reach podium at Europeans in 15 years with 2007 silver

• Trains with Carolina Kostner in Oberstdorf

• Older brother Miroslav competed in pairs as a junior

Kiira Korpi

Born: September 26, 1988

Hometown: Tampere, Finland

Training site: Tampere

Coaches: Maaret Siromaa, Susanna Haarala

Choreographers: Nelli Petänen

- Kiira won her first major ISU medal with a bronze at 2007 Europeans

- In 2006–07: 6th, Cup of Russia; 7th, Skate America; 14th, Worlds (after 10th in '06)

- Her father, Rauno, coached Finnish women's hockey team to bronze at 1998 Olympics

European crown of his career. Tomas Verner, the stylish Czech, won the short program when Joubert missed his quad-toe combination, but was no match for the Grand Prix champion in the freeskate. Joubert entered the event worrying about the pressure caused by world champion Stéphane Lambiel's withdrawal, which left him as overwhelming favorite. That kind of distraction might have weighed too heavily on him in the past, but he had spent the entire fall season building confidence. Lambiel had withdrawn from competition since Skate Canada, claiming he was out of shape and had lost his drive.

Verner won the silver medal, and Belgium's veteran Kevin van der Perren finished second in the freeskate to claim the bronze medal. Van der Perren had finished 28th in the 2000 Europeans as an 18-year-old and made slow progress before finally reaching the podium. He was the first Belgian man to win a medal at Europeans in 50 years, extending the new trend of smaller skating nations breaking long medal droughts.

That trend extends to Italy and long-suffering Finland in the women's division. Three of the top six finishers at 2007 Europeans were from Finland. Kiira Korpi, who had missed practice time after a September injury, finished only fourth at Finnish Nationals but rallied from fifth in the short program to finish third and win her first major international medal. The graceful skater, whose classic carriage is often compared to Grace Kelly's, finished well back of second-place Sarah Meier. The Swiss champion had arrived as prohibitive favorite after finishing third in the Grand Prix Final. Susanna Pöykiö of Finland was fourth and compatriot Alisa Drei moved up from ninth to finish sixth. Pöykiö, the four-time national champion, was the first Finnish woman to medal at an ISU championship with her bronze at the 2001 Junior Worlds. Her 2005 silver was the first-ever Finnish medal in women's singles at the European championships.

But the story of the week was the spectacular

Susanna Pöykiö

Born: February 22, 1982

Hometown: Oulu, Finland

Training site: Oulu

Coach: Heidi Pöykiö

Choreographers: Megan Smith-Gage; Outi Martikainen

- Susanna, Kiira Korpi, and junior Jenni Vähämaa lead a revival of Finnish skating
- In 2006–07: 5th, Skate Canada and Trophée Eric Bompard; 4th, Europeans; 8th, Worlds
- First Finnish woman to medal at Europeans (silver, 2005)
- Is now coached by older sister Heidi

return of Italy's Carolina Kostner. She missed the entire 2006–07 Grand Prix series with torn ankle ligaments, and said she came into Warsaw "feeling like an outsider because I hadn't competed." For Kostner maybe that was a good thing. She had felt intense pressure during the Olympic season after becoming the first Italian woman to medal at Worlds with her bronze in 2005.

Kostner, who comes from a family of incredibly accomplished athletes, vowed to stay more relaxed

ITA

Carolina Kostner

Born: February 8, 1987

Hometown: Ortisei, Italy

Training site: Oberstdorf, Germany

Coach: Michael Huth

Choreographer: Lori Nichol

- Missed the entire 2006–07 Grand Prix series due to torn ankle ligaments; came back to win Europeans and finish 6th at Worlds

- First Italian woman ever to win Europeans, and first to medal at Worlds (bronze, 2005) in 29 years

- First Italian singles skater to medal at Junior Worlds (2003)

- An incredible family of athletes: father Erwin played hockey in Olympics; mother Patrizia was nationally ranked skater; cousin Isolde was World Cup downhill ski champion

after her ninth-place finish at the 2006 Olympics and she followed her own advice, not allowing a missed jump to affect her first-place freeskating performance. That allowed her to move past Meier and become the first Italian woman ever to win the European championships.

While Italy celebrated, Russia mourned. It failed

to win a men's medal for the first time since 1999. So while some droughts were broken, a major oasis had gone dry.

Four Continents

The European championships earn respect beyond their current relevance, but the Four Continents championships suffer from the opposite effect. The event debuted in 1999, as the supposed equivalent to Europeans, giving skaters from the other continents equal access to prize money, judges and an international tune-up before Worlds. At one time, it was predicted that the Europeans and Four Continents might serve as qualifying rounds for the Worlds, but the idea did not fly with the smaller nations.

The Four Continents has never caught on with TV or live audiences, particularly in North America, where minuscule crowds threaten its very existence. The International Skating Union has considered canceling the money-eater, but for the 2006–07 season it was given a boost by the new bonus for yearly points standings. Any top skater who skips the Four Continents not only doesn't have a chance at the $15,000 first prize, but is also unlikely to qualify for season-ending bonuses.

Most eligible nations try to send quality skaters to the Four Continents, but the main reason for crowd apathy is that the United States has rarely sent its best singles skaters, the household names who attract ticket-buyers. Even when the 2001 Four Continents served as the test event for the 2002 Olympic venue at Salt Lake City, the American team was thin.

However, in 2007, for the first time all current American champions competed at Four Continents. Crowds were still very small, but for the most part the entry list was solid.

Evan Lysacek rode into Colorado Springs on a wave of momentum from his first U.S. championship and exhibited exactly the right approach. A dedicated trainer and feisty competitor, he rallied from fourth in the short program to win the title, but that

Jeremy Abbott

CAN

Jeffrey Buttle

Born: September 1, 1982

Hometown: Smooth Rock Falls, Ontario

Training sites: Barrie, Ontario;
Lake Arrowhead California

Coaches: Lee Barkell; Rafael Aratunian

Choreographer: David Wilson

- Jeff's back injury kept him out of 2006–07 competition until Nationals

- In 2006–07: Won third national title; 6th, Worlds; 2nd, Four Continents

- 2nd, 2005 Worlds

- Brilliant 2005–06 season: 3rd, Olympics; 2nd, Grand Prix Final, 1st, Trophée Eric Bompard; 2nd, Skate Canada

- Studies chemical engineering at University of Toronto

- Did competitive dance and ice dancing with sister Meghan

was secondary to his main goal of making "the quadruple-triple combination just like any other jump, so it won't seem like a new thing anymore." Although he two-footed his quad, he went at it with gusto. The more it's landed, even partially, the more it eases into his overall choreography.

Canadian Jeffrey Buttle, still taking precautionary therapy for his autumn back problems, was as brilliant as ever in his spins and footwork but struggled in jumps and finished second. The big thrill for the small audiences, though, was the third- and fourth-place finishes of, respectively, Jeremy Abbott and Ryan Bradley. Both train in Colorado Springs at the famous Broadmoor Skating Club, and Abbott's second-place short program was the highlight of the week for many local fans. He was born and raised in Colorado, and it was his first senior international medal.

Kimmie Meissner also displayed a fighting spirit, moving from sixth in the short program to the top of the podium, buoyed by her early triple Lutz–triple toe combination. Emily Hughes skated a clean long program for a personal best in points, a good sign heading into Worlds, and finished second overall.

After her strong first-place short program, Canadian champion Joannie Rochette could not conquer either of her triple Lutzes and dropped to third. This time it was Japan that didn't send its best singles team, with none of its three World team women in attendance. The rising power's top finish was Aki Sawada's fourth place.

Four Continents provided a perfect opportunity for American dance champions Tanith Belbin and Ben Agosto to add more competitive miles to their brand new *Amélie* freedance. Belbin admitted that playing a serious character after years "of being told to smile and smile" required some adjustment. They won the silver behind Canadians Marie-France Dubreuil and Patrice Lauzon, but lost by less than two points.

The Canadians were making their first appearance at Four Continents in three years, and it was their

Evan Lysacek

JPN

Aki Sawada

Born: October 7, 1988

Hometown: Osaka, Japan

Training site: Kyoto, Japan

Coaches: Mie Hamada; Yamato Tamura

Choreographer: Tom Dickson

- As a first-year senior in 2007, was 6th in the competitive Japanese Nationals
- In 2006–07: 5th, Cup of Russia, 8th, Cup of China; 4th, Four Continents
- Has landed triple Axels at Nationals

Emily Hughes

first victory there, continuing an impressive season. The tight battle for the bronze between two younger teams, won by Canada's Tessa Virtue and Scott Moir over the U.S. duo of Meryl Davis and Charlie White, solidified a new era for ice dancing. With little competition from other countries, all 27 ice dance medals in the nine-year history of the Four Continents have been won by couples from Canada or the United States, but the difference heading into the 2010 Games is that all three medalists, plus the pewter medalist (fourth), are legitimate hopes for the podium at the Olympics. What a change in just a couple of years!

The lingering image of the 2007 Four Continents, however, was a more negative one and a graphic reminder that pairs is not only the most hazardous of the four figure skating disciplines, but also one of the most dangerous pursuits in all of sport.

Xue Shen and Hongbo Zhao, coming directly from the Asian Games, extended their undefeated streak despite their fatigue. Battered teammates Qing Pang and Jian Tong — she had after-effects from an autumn kidney ailment, and he was sporting a 12-stitch scar from being hit by a car in January — finished second. Rena Inoue and

Ryan Bradley

Born: November 17, 1983

Hometown: St. Joseph, Missouri

Training site: Colorado Springs, Colorado

Coach: Tom Zakrajsek

Choreographers: Caterina Lindgren; Nikolai Morozov

• In 2006–07, won his first medal (silver) at Nationals; made his Worlds debut (15th); 4th on home ice at Four Continents in Colorado Springs

• Competed in pairs (Tiffany Vise), 1997–98

John Baldwin, the defending champions, gave themselves encouragement for Worlds by landing their trademark throw triple Axel.

But early in the freeskate final, there was a near-tragedy involving new Canadian champions Jessica Dubé and Bryce Davison. They hadn't skated well in the short, but were off to an impressive start in their freeskate. One of their distinctive traits is close proximity on spins and jumps. But as they went into their flying camel spins, they seemed to be a bit too close together. On the third rotation, Davison's skate blade — estimated by some to be traveling at a tangential speed of at least 25 miles per hour — struck Dubé in the face. Her head recoiled from the impact and she dropped to the ice as blood began pooling around her. The shocked audience held its collective breath. Even seasoned observers have trouble watching the replay, which was shown dozens of times on Canadian and U.S. TV shows.

If there is such a thing as being lucky in such horrific circumstances, Dubé was. The skate missed her eye, her temple and her jugular vein, but it did slice the left side of her face from her upper cheek right into her nose. She was rushed to a local hospital and underwent emergency plastic surgery. But the very next day she watched a video of the accident and also suggested that she wanted to compete at Worlds. Ten days later, she and Davison briefly skated together during a practice session for the 100th anniversary celebration of the London (Ontario) Figure Skating Club, an event they were originally scheduled to headline. The first thing they did in practice was the side-by-side camel spins — in effect, jumping right back on the horse that had thrown them.

"Definitely," Davison told the *Hamilton Spectator,* "doing those camel spins the first time again was difficult. As an athlete, though, you have to go at it and not think in the past. We've done them so many times, and this happened once. It could happen again, yes, but you don't think about it, you can't."

Later, in front of the full audience at London's

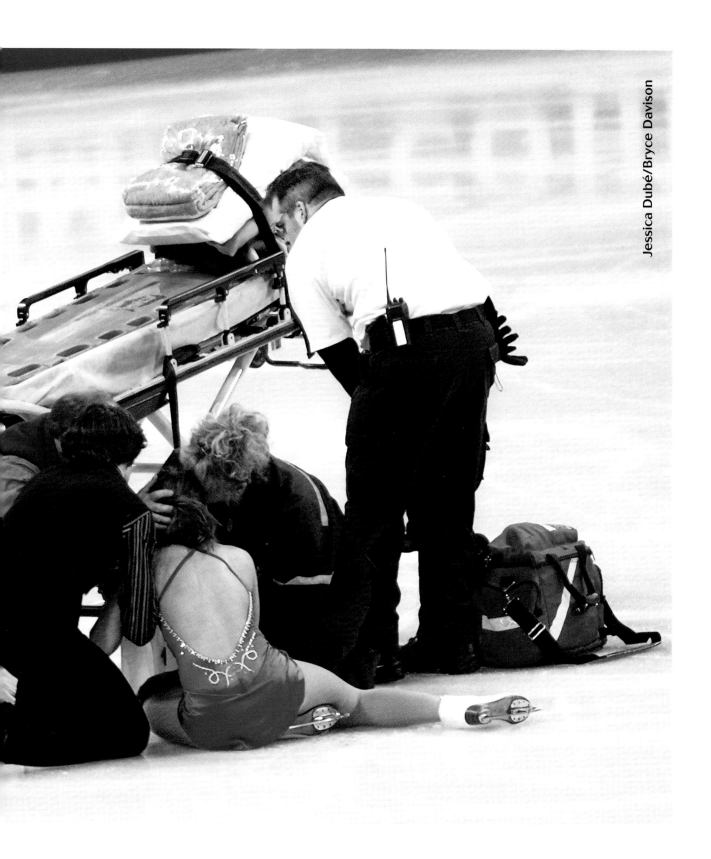

Dan Zhang/Hao Zhang (left)

Jessica Dubé/Bryce Davison

John Labatt Centre, they performed a few routine moves, and then did the flying camel spins. Long before they finished the spins the knowledgeable crowd jumped to its feet in heartfelt appreciation of what the pair had endured.

While the physical aftermath of a bad pairs injury is difficult, the psychological backlash is usually worse. One partner or the other, or both, can fear the offending element to the point of phobia; there can be a severe decline in self-confidence; or trust between partners can be eroded. Elena Berezhnaya never skated again with Oleg Shliakhov after his skate became embedded in her head in 1996, on a flying camel spin, sending her into a coma and

impeding her speech for months. Olympic silver medalist Debbi Wilkes never again performed a certain lift she had fallen from during a photo shoot in the early 1960s.

But pairs also can survive awful accidents to go on to win medals, as Dan Zhang did with her partner Hao Zhang in the 2006 Olympics. Tatiana Totmianina came back from a terrible fall at Skate America in 2004, to win the world title with Maxim Marinin four months later.

Dubé, like most pairs women, is used to recovering from accident and injury. But she's endured more than most. She lost half a finger in an early-childhood accident, has incurred numerous

Tatiana Totmianina

other injuries, suffered a bad fall before the 2006–07 season and also required arthroscopic surgery on her knee in September 2006.

"She is unbelievably tough," Davison said. "Look at what she has overcome."

And rather than ignore the accident and merely hope that there would be no future psychological roadblocks, the pair looked it right in the eye, enlisting the aid of a sports psychologist and a post-trauma psychologist near Montreal.

"We have watched that video replay a number, a great number, of times," Davison said later. "The psychologist said watching it would help and it has. We now see it as an accident, with no blame. It's to the point where we're not insensitive but we can handle it."

And that was exactly what they needed to enable them to join the rest of the global elite at the final, most prestigious event of the skating season: the world championships.

Jessica Dubé/Bryce Davison

Miki Ando

Springing to Worlds

The World Figure Skating Championships are the highlight of the season for the planet's best singles skaters, pairs and ice dancers. But there are two lesser-known official world championships that are just as important to those who are eligible — Junior Worlds, and the World Synchronized Skating Championships.

Junior Worlds

The world junior championships are often an advance preview of what's to come at the highest level. Current Olympic-level luminaries who have won Junior Worlds include Mao Asada, Miki Ando, Nobunari Oda, Yu-Na Kim, Daisuke Takahashi, Johnny Weir, Tanith Belbin and Ben Agosto, and Tessa Virtue and Scott Moir.

In early March 2007 at Oberstdorf, Germany, Stephen Carriere became the first American man to win the global under-19 championship since Weir and Evan Lysacek finished one-two six years earlier. Carriere jumped to the title all the way from a sixth-place standing after the short program.

The men's leader after the short program, Patrick Chan, dropped to second but still won Canada's first Junior Worlds men's medal in 23 years. Chan, 16, was enduring the first season of his skating life without legendary Osborne Colson as his coach. The charismatic Colson, whom Chan treated like a grandfather, died the previous summer at the age of 90 with the Chan family at his bedside. Chan wears a gold medallion that belonged to Colson.

On the women's side, it was the first podium sweep for the United States in the 32-year history of Junior Worlds.

Caroline Zhang beat Mirai Nagasu for the gold medal, avenging her loss to Nagasu at U.S. Junior Nationals. Ashley Wagner took home the bronze medal. Zhang and Nagasu were only 13 years old

---

Top to bottom: Miki Ando, Mao Asada, Brian Joubert

USA

Stephen Carriere

Born: June 15, 1989

Hometown: Wakefield, Massachusetts

Training site: Boston, Massachusetts

Coaches: Peter Johansson; Mark Mitchell

Choreographer: Jamie Isley

• Landed eight triples to move from 6th to 1st in the 2007 Junior Worlds

• Was inspired to skate by watching Nancy Kerrigan, who was from his area, at 1994 Olympics

USA

Caroline Zhang

Born: May 20, 1993

Hometown: Irvine, California

Training sites: Lakewood and Artesia, California

Coaches: Mingzhu Li; Sandra Holmes

Choreographer: Cindy Stuart

• Won the 2007 world junior championship, leading the first-ever U.S. sweep of the podium

• Two of the other three U.S. 13-year-olds to win Junior Worlds were Michelle Kwan and Elaine Zayak, who became world champions. The third, Tiffany Chin, finished 3rd twice

CAN

Patrick Chan

Born: December 31, 1990

Hometown: Toronto, Ontario

Training site: Toronto, Ontario

Coaches: Shin Amano; Don Laws

Choreographer: Lori Nichol

• Moved steadily up the world junior ranks — from 7th in 2005, to 6th in 2006, to the silver medal in 2007

• An avid pianist and a good scholar, he speaks three languages fluently

during Junior Worlds, which bodes well for the future of American skating.

World Synchronized Skating Championships

A week or two after the Senior Worlds, the increasingly popular World Synchronized Skating Championships take the stage.

Synchronized skating didn't get its first official world championship until 1998, although there had been an unofficial global event the two previous seasons.

Skating's ultimate team game, which was once known as precision skating, has grown rapidly, and almost unrecognizably, from its origins rooted in the marching bands of the American midwest. The 2007 world championships, held at the 12,000-seat John Labatt Centre in London, Ontario, were a cornucopia of sight and sound

and had been sold out for four months before the actual event.

Although there had been various types of group skating in England, Ottawa and New York in the early 1900s, the acknowledged birthplace of modern synchronized skating was a college town in Michigan. In the early 1960s, Dr. Richard Porter of the Ann Arbor Skating Club grew concerned about the migration of teenaged girls away from the testing and competitive streams, so he formed the Hockettes skating team to keep the older girls and women interested in the sport. The name was a play upon the Radio City Music Hall Rockettes, the famous kick-line chorus, and also upon the team's regular performances during intermissions of University of Michigan hockey games.

Synchronized skating quickly evolved from its marching band motif and developed a unique, more demanding, form of its own. It crossed over

The Hockettes

92

Team Nexxice

the Canadian border and took root in southwestern Ontario. It had a familiar feel because group routines had always been part of the popular club carnivals. The sport spread rapidly, and in 1979 Canada held its first national championships in Ilderton, just north of London. So in 2007, the sport had come full geographic circle in Canada.

Synchronized skating has become so demanding that Skate Canada had to establish two tiers of regional and national championships, because to be an elite synchronized skater now requires nearly as much commitment as it does to be a top singles skater. The 2007 Canadian champions, Nexxice, are based in two Ontario rinks in Waterloo and Burlington, which are about 40 miles apart, and the team practices five times or more per week.

The rules were tightened up in the mid-1990s because of safety concerns, but since then the

Marigold Ice Unity

94

Team Surprise

sport has moved in a more high-risk direction. The footwork is far more exacting, the speed has increased dramatically, the choreography has become intricate and even more visually stunning, and in recent years, certain pairs lifts have been allowed.

While there were 21 teams (some including male skaters) representing 16 nations at the 2007 world championships, the undisputed leader of the sport remains Team Surprise from Sweden. The Swedes have won all but three world titles, finishing second to Finland's Marigold Ice Unity each of those times, and won again decisively in 2007. They capped the frenetic weekend with a brilliant freeskate, which sent the arena into a delirious, thumping roar, and resulted in a record 144.70 points.

The ascending Nexxice, led by renowned coach Shelley Barnett, won its first world medal and Canada's first in four years when it took bronze, while the other Canadian entry, Montreal's Les Suprêmes, finished sixth.

And, for the first time, a U.S. team found itself on the world podium. Miami University Redhawks, the first U.S. synchronized team to be accorded official varsity sport status, won the silver medal. Another traditionally strong American team, the Haydenettes, just missed the medals with a fourth-place standing to give the United States its best combined finish ever, and the best of any country at the 2007 world championships. That should help spur more U.S. interest in the sport, which already has a hipper, more raucous ambience to its championships than skating's other disciplines.

The World Championships

While the once manic support for figure skating has declined in the United States and western Europe, it is on a sharp rise in the east.

So, it was fitting that the first Worlds of the new Olympiad would be held in Tokyo, Japan, with several of the favorites in singles events — Yu-Na

Daisuke Takahashi

Kim, Mao Asada, Daisuke Takahashi and Nubanari Oda — coming from the east.

"It is the result of the culture," Lee Barkell, the Canadian half of Oda's coaching tandem, explained to Canadian TV. "Hard work is the only way to go."

The 2007 global championship was radically different from most Worlds in the past, but likely not from those in the future. No one could ever remember a world championship in which all four reigning champions were returning to defend their titles, but not one of them as the favorite. That, though, was the case in Tokyo.

A large reason for this oddity, which is about to become commonplace, is the success of skating's relatively new International Judging System. The IJS was built to reward skaters for their performance that

Stéphane Lambiel

So, in 2007, the defending world champions all faced at least one competitor who seemed more likely to win than they did.

In the women's division, Kimmie Meissner had won the Four Continents and her first national title, but didn't have a victory on the Grand Prix circuit. Grand Prix Final winner Yu-Na Kim and the sensational Mao Asada, two 16 year olds in their first season of Worlds eligibility, were annointed as favorites.

In dance, 2006 winners Albena Denkova and Maxim Staviski were enjoying a fine farewell season until they finished third at Europeans. And Canadian stars Marie-France Dubreuil and Patrice Lauzon were not even in that event.

In pairs, defending champions Qing Pang and Jian Tong endured injury and health problems all year — she had a kidney illness, and he wore a headband at Worlds to hide the 12-stitch scar from being hit by a car midway through the competitive season. And icons Xue Shen and Hongbo Zhao, who had missed 2006 Worlds, had beaten them every time out.

Two-time men's world champion Stéphane Lambiel was resuming competition for the first time since early November, after pondering his focus and his future. "It was very important for me to understand that figure skating is my life and what I want to do," the likeable Swiss said upon his return. "This is a good challenge, but I have no pressure on me."

That pressure had transferred itself directly to the shoulders of European champion Brian Joubert of France, who had not handled such weight well in the past. With a chance to win in Moscow in 2005, he bombed his long program, and during the Olympic season he felt overburdened, and therefore too tight to compete well. But developing a freer sense of choreography with Kurt Browning, one of the great rise-to-the-occasion skaters of the late 1980s and early 1990s, and enjoying his most successful season to date had made Joubert more

very day, not in the past. Another factor is the depth and breadth of the competitive season, which creates better competitors, provides a barometer of season-long trends and, on the negative side, contributes to more injuries. Yet another cause is the rise of once weak skating nations, fueled by the migration of eastern European coaches to other countries, and the reverse migration of international skaters to Canada, the United States and, sometimes, Russia for training facilities and coaching.

Qing Pang/Jian Tong

Brian Joubert

through (in front of the demanding French media) only a week before leaving for Tokyo.

It was a new Joubert at 2007 Worlds. He not only won the short program with ease, but he also fended off the nerves that mount in the two days before the freeskate and opened with an impressive quadruple jump. Knowing that a clean skate would likely earn him his first world title, Joubert, who had done three quads in his freeskate in earlier competition, downgraded a quad combination to a triple toe–triple toe. The conservative skate didn't have the electricity he's capable of generating, but he maintained his composure and didn't melt down. He finished a careful third in the freeskate, but that was enough to give him his world championship and France's first since 1965, when the smooth Alain Calmat, who was in the audience in Tokyo, won France's only other men's title. Joubert also shed the label nobody wants: best skater not to win a world title.

"It wasn't my best. I gave everything I have tonight, but I can do better," he conceded. "But it has been a great season. My next big goal is the Olympics in 2010. It did not work out for me in 2006, and I do not want that to happen again. I am so relieved with this title. Waiting for the scores in the freeskate was just torture."

It was also torture for the North American men. Evan Lysacek, to his credit, kept at his quads, which was one of his primary goals, but missed the podium for the first time in three years, finishing fifth. Johnny Weir, who'd had an excellent short program to stand fourth, dropped all the way to eighth, landing only four triples. Emanuel Sandhu, who had been fifth only the year before, struggled badly throughout the week and finished 16th overall, scoring 61 points lower than he had in 2006. Jeffrey Buttle, whose season never really began until January beacause of a bad back, stood second after the short. The Olympic bronze medalist attempted a quadruple jump in the freeskate, under-rotated it and fell, finishing sixth

confident. Browning would say later that he wished he could have spent even more time with Joubert to unleash a larger cache of his great potential.

Joubert, though, had injured tendons a few weeks before Worlds, when he drove his left skate into his right foot during training. To protect the injury he refrained from practicing his triple flips and Lutzes, and did his first full program run-for the second succesive Worlds. If a skater must try, under any circumstances, to get an inconsistent element under control, it is at the Worlds three years removed from the next Olympics.

Buttle had the misfortune of skating after Daisuke Takahashi, who had ignited the crowd with his freeskate, the finest performance of the evening. Other terrific skates went to the surprising Stéphane Lambiel who, although clearly rusty, took home the bronze; and to Tomas Verner, who turned in the best freeskate of his career. Verner was the only skater to land two quads in the freeskate and he nailed a late triple Axel as well, jumping all the way from ninth to fourth overall. This came just two years after he failed to make it out of the qualifying round.

There were nine accredited quad jumps in the men's finale, and another half-dozen attempts, signaling that the four-revolution leap will be an absolute prerequisite for Vancouver in 2010.

One of the near-misses, though, was part of the most thrilling men's freeskate in years. Daisuke Takahashi touched a hand to the ice on his quadruple jump, but used that strong opening as a springboard to a vibrant performance which drew the overflow crowd's thunderous approval. Takahashi broke down and sobbed for several minutes after winning the freeskate and the silver medal, Japan's best finish ever. It was a brilliant, satisfying moment for him, the partisan audience and his entire country. Takahashi had survived and prevailed over unimagineable media pressure and the expectations of an entire nation.

In pairs, Xue Shen and Hongbo Zhao were coy about whether they would return for the 2010 Olympics, but they were certainly going to skip the 2007–08 season and will likely remain retired. If so, they went out on top. Their short program, perhaps their last, was the highest-scoring of their sparkling careers. When they finished their freeskate, clearly the winners, Zhao knelt down, partly to touch the ice in appreciation to Japan for always being such a great host to him and his partner, but mostly to

propose marriage to Xue Shen. She knelt too, at first misunderstanding what he was up to. Later, they formally announced their engagement.

He kissed her on the right cheek, a far more intimate act than the two had ever been permitted to show in public. And they skated to the Kiss 'n' Cry to a standing ovation celebrating their marvelous careers. It had been a long journey from the frigid

Daisuke Takahashi

Xue Shen/Hongbo Zhao

102

outdoor conditions in Harbin, where as a child Shen had skated until her feet bled. That journey included the rigid discipline of the national training center; the pair's heartbreaking injuries and early awkwardness with spins and choreography; and the forced keeping-apart of a young couple who — so obvious to the rest of the skating world — were in love. Finally, it took them to the top of the podium, and with it worldwide awe and respect.

Their successors, at home and abroad, will be either Qing Pang and Jian Tong, who were second in Tokyo, or Dan Zhang and Hao Zhang, who finished fifth. But bronze medalists Germans Aliona Savchenko and Robin Szolkowy, who had a tremendous year despite the stress caused by the German Olympic Committee's disfavor with their

Aliona Savchenko/Robin Szolkowy

Dan Zhang/Hao Zhang

coach Ingo Steuer, will be a threat all the way to Vancouver 2010. And Ukraine's Tatiana Volosozhar and Stanislav Morozov also showed they're poised to challenge for the rest of the Olympiad, moving from eighth after the short program to fourth overall.

For traditionally pairs-strong Canada and the hopeful United States, 2007 was not a happy world championship.

Valerie Marcoux and Craig Buntin (sixth), Jessica Dubé and Bryce Davison (seventh), and newcomers Anabelle Langlois and Cody Hay (tenth) all coped with a variety of troubles. But with their finish, Canada managed to qualify three pairs for the 2008 Worlds, which would relieve some stress at Nationals. A month after Worlds, Marcoux announced her retirement from competitive skating and decided to enter the coaching ranks. "Valerie is the most positive, perservering and fiercely competitive person I have ever met," Buntin said. "I have no doubt we will remain close friends for the rest of our lives."

Marie-France Dubreuil/Patrice Lauzon

Rena Inoue and John Baldwin had trouble in the freeskate with their brand name, the throw triple Axel, as they did much of the season. They finished eighth. New American champions Brooke Castile and Benjamin Okolski were 12th in their debut Worlds, partly due to her stomach flu.

And it was farewell to respected Dorota and Mariusz Siudek. But the only Polish pair ever to medal at Worlds never got the chance to take a final bow as they had to withdraw because of his back injury, incurred just before the freeskate.

Another drought-breaking European team also said goodbye as dancers Albena Denkova and Maxim Staviski, the first Bulgarians ever to medal and win at Worlds, recovered from their poor Europeans performance to win a second straight championship. Snubbed by the judges for years during dancing's dark days of deception, the talented Bulgarians exited with four world medals and were the only 2006 champions to repeat in 2007.

"This is the brilliant end for us," Staviski said.

They edged disappointed Canadians Marie-France Dubreuil and Patrice Lauzon by a mere 1.15 points, but that slim margin was twice as wide as the difference in 2006. A different set of judges might have seen it another way … or they might not have.

With Tanith Belbin and Ben Agosto picking up the bronze medal (by a thin 0.24 points over Isabelle Delobel and Olivier Schoenfelder), despite a fourth place finish in the freedance, the podium placings were the same as the previous year. But unlike the pre-2005 ice dance world, the results were not decided entirely by protocol and politics.

"This is what we wanted, that there would be good judging in the competition. And we got it," Dubreuil philosophized. "So we cannot complain."

Sixth-place finishers Tessa Virtue and Scott Moir of Canada and seventh-place Meryl Davis and Charlie White of the United States gave North America four of the top seven placings, a political impossibility just three years earlier. Underscoring

Isabelle Delobel/Olivier Schoenfelder

the value of the new judging system, the young North American couples each moved up three places from their compulsory dances, and also provided the best Worlds debut by an American dance team in 27 years and by a Canadian couple in 40 years.

That highlighted a sea change in ice dancing that is just as stunning as the power shift in women's singles.

The women's world championship — still officially called "ladies" by the ISU — is always the final event of the Olympic-eligible season. It can be a difficult and pressure-packed wait for the women, especially now that the early-week qualifying rounds have been discarded. However,

the elimination of the "Q" round should mean better overall competition in the long run because the top athletes will have more left in the tank for the finale.

Brian Orser, returning as a participant to the Worlds for the first time as Yu Na Kim's coach, was amazed at the depth of the women's field, which he said "has terrific skaters all the way right down to the top 12."

But the excited audiences at the Tokyo Metropolitan Gymnasium were focusing mainly on the three Japanese women (Mao Asada, Miki Ando and Yukari Nakano), South Korea's Kim, and reigning world champion Kimmie Meissner of the United States.

Because of the quality and quantity of upper-tier skaters, it was going to require not only a high degree of technical accomplishment — most of the top women had triple-triple combinations in their arsenal — but also some refined artistry to win the world title. It would also take solid performances in both the short program and freeskate.

Kim was the star of the short program, demonstrating not only that her Grand Prix Final victory was no accident but also that she had overcome the bulging disks in her back which had plagued her all year. She set a new world's best with a sensational 71.95 points, surpassing Sasha Cohen's 71.12, which had stood for nearly four years.

Miki Ando, somewhat overshadowed in the tidal wave of publicity surrounding the younger Kim and Mao Asada, was just three points back in second place after the short program. Italy's Carolina Kostner, flying below the pre-Worlds radar despite her surprise victory at Europeans, stood third and Kimmie Meissner was fourth. Mao Asada, in her first skate at Worlds, was a disappointing fifth, a result that would cost her dearly.

The top four women in the short program all landed triple-triple combinations, confirming that this is indeed a new high-risk era.

In the freeskate, Kim started well and seemed

Tanith Belbin/Ben Agosto

Miki Ando

Kimmie Meissner

headed toward a championship, but she tumbled on both her triple Lutzes midway through her program — falls had been her only stumbling block all season — which sent her to fourth in the freeskate, and third overall. Still, it was a brilliant Worlds debut.

She was followed directly by the other 16-year-old wunderkind, Mao Asada, who opened with a triple Axel attempt that was only slightly two-footed. The crowd reacted like thunder and they kept roaring right through Asada's fabulous presentation. By the time she did her high-level flying sit spin at the

111

Miki Ando

end, the crowd was already on its feet, screaming in pleasure. Asada reacted emotionally, and cried again at her personal best score of 133.13. "I love skating at home," she understated.

Kimmie Meissner had the misfortune of skating directly after Asada while the cheering still reverberated through the arena. As befitted her season of highs and lows, she had good moments and some weak ones in the freeskate and dropped to fourth place overall.

That left Ando as the only skater who could beat Asada. She had a lead of 6.56 points over Asada after the short so she could skate relatively conservatively, but could not afford any mistakes. The pressure was enormous, especially since she could hear the reaction her countrywoman had created.

Ando had some wobbly landings but did manage to land seven triples, and did not attempt

the quadruple Salchow on which she had fallen at the Olympics. That fall had sent her all the way down to 15th place. She had carried the weight of disappointment all season.

But Ando showed tremendous poise despite her nervousness, and supplemented her triples with high-level combination spins and some excellent footwork. The performance lacked the punch and electricity that Asada had shown, but Ando finished second in the freeskate and won the gold medal by less than seven-tenths of a point.

As Ando's scores and placement flashed on the scoreboard, Asada seemed temporarily stunned. When Ando realized that she was the new world champion, she hugged her coach Nikolai Morozov and could not stop sobbing.

"I can't find words to express my feelings," the gold medalist said through tears. "There were

Mao Asada

Miki Ando (center)

people who criticized my selection for the Olympics and I had a difficult time because of that. But thanks to my family and coaches, I came back strong."

And strong is the perfect adjective to describe women's skating in Asia. Japanese skaters finished first, second and fifth, and a South Korean was third. Only fourth-place Kimmie Meissner, who had been world champion, broke the Asian domination. It was the first time in 13 years that no American woman had stood on the world podium.

In a far less publicized triumph much farther down the standings, Joannie Rochette jumped from 16th after the short program to 10th overall with a very strong fifth-place freeskate. That meant that Canada could send two women to the 2008 Worlds, extremely important for a proud skating country

trying to develop a discipline in which it has gone 20 world championships without a medal.

It would take only a few days after Worlds until skaters were thinking about and planning for the next season. And two years beyond it.

Word had already leaked out that 2006 Olympic men's champion Evgeny Plushenko, missing the competitive environment, was planning a return for the 2007–08 season. He, like Sasha Cohen, had Vancouver on his mind.

"After seeing the result of Russian skating in Tokyo I want to help," said Plushenko. "I feel strongly that I can be competitive and ready for the 2010 Olympics."

Which is exactly what dozens of other skaters are telling themselves as they head full of hope toward the Vancouver Games.

Shizuka Arakawa

Figure Skating in Japan:
A New Era *by Akiko Tamura*

"I think that figure skating gained its citizenship in Japan only recently — probably a year before the Olympics in Torino," says Hiromitsu Okude, who works for Kyodo News, a leading news agency in Japan. What Okude means is that until now, figure skating wasn't given much attention by the Japanese media. Unlike baseball, soccer or even speed skating, it wasn't taken seriously as a sport.

In 1992, the Japanese media was criticized for putting pressure on Midori Ito at the Albertville Olympics. To be fair, the hype was nowhere near what Nancy Kerrigan received at Lillehammer in 1994, and didn't compare with what Michelle Kwan had to deal with throughout her competitive years. But at that time, Japanese skaters were simply not used to being in the limelight. Although there had been world championship medalists like Minoru Sano (1977 men's bronze) and Emi Watanabe (1979 women's bronze), Midori Ito was probably the first

Japanese figure skater to establish a name that extended beyond the country's skating fans. But when she retired from competition after winning the silver medal in Albertville, a long period followed in which figure skating barely mattered to the general public. Even when Yuka Sato won the world title in 1994, things didn't much change.

The interest slowly returned when Takeshi Honda and Fumie Suguri won the world bronze medals — each won twice, in 2002 and 2003. That's when Japan began to notice that its skaters were once again becoming competitive on an international level.

But it was Miki Ando with her quadruple jumps — the first ever done competitively by a woman — who really made the headlines. "We always had a certain number of die-hard figure skating fans in Japan," Okude explained. "They were mainly young women following foreign male skaters. But Miki reached out to a totally different, much wider crowd. She's a pretty girl, a next-door type, and

Top to bottom: Miki Ando, Mao Asada, Daisuke Takahashi

Takeshi Honda

is capable of doing jumps that no other woman had done. She appealed to people who had never before watched skating." Miki was photogenic and the media adored her. Toyota, originally based in Nagoya-City, where Miki is from, offered her a sponsorship. When her commercial aired on TV in January 2005, it was the first major such appearance by any figure skater in Japan. And it was only a beginning.

Next it was Mao Asada who stole the spotlight. In the 2006 Grand Prix Final in Tokyo, the 15-year-old became an overnight sensation after beating then world champion Irina Slutskaya. Mao was offered several endorsements, and one company even created stuffed animals based on her dog, Aero, who appeared in a commercial alongside its owner. An adorable young girl, Mao had a story that the media loved: she had beaten the best in the world, yet was too young to compete in the Olympics. Although they knew better, a number of tabloids criticized the Japanese Skating Federation for not pushing the International Skating Union enough to make an exception for Mao and allow her to compete in Torino.

But there was a surprising, happy ending to this story. In the Olympics, Shizuka Arakawa won the gold medal, the first one ever by a figure skater from Asia. Shizuka gained immediate stardom, and skating's popularity soared. The fact that she was the only Japanese medalist in Torino didn't hurt, either. Shizuka was showered with opportunities never before heard of in the Japanese skating world. She became a guest commentator at the soccer World Cup in 2006, found herself modeling on a fashion runway, and was invited to see the opera *Turandot* — she had skated to its music at the Olympics — with the Japanese prime minister. She also appeared in various ice shows, including a charity show for young skaters that she organized herself. Nearly every performance sold out. For the first time in the country's history, figure skating was hot.

Even without Shizuka competing, the 2007

Worlds in Tokyo proved a huge success. Tickets sold out in two minutes. A ticket for the ladies' freeskate was offered on a Yahoo Japan auction, and is said to have sold for 150,000 yen (about $1,250). The Fuji TV network, which covered the championships exclusively in Japan, scored a 38.1 percent rating for the ladies' freeskate and hit 51.18 percent when Miki Ando won her event. Three medals at Worlds — Miki's gold, Mao Asada's silver and Daisuke

Midori Ito

Nobunari Oda

Takahashi's silver in men's — set a record for Japan. Over 200 members of the Japanese media covered the event.

The success of Japanese skaters seemed inevitable when a young generation began to reach the podium at the Junior Worlds a few years earlier. Yukina Ota won the ladies' title in 2003, Miki Ando in 2004 and Mao Asada in 2005. As for the men, Daisuke Takahashi won in 2002, Nobunari Oda in 2005 and Takahiko Kozuka in 2006. But the question is, how long will all this last?

The United States, Canada and Russia have all experienced their highs and lows in figure skating. Japan is certainly now hitting its peak. But some observers are concerned that none of the country's skaters reached the podium at the 2007 Junior Worlds. Rumi Suizu, finishing fifth among the women, was the country's top skater. Miki and Mao will skate their way to the Vancouver Olympics, but what about the generation that follows them?

Some believe that part of the problem involves the resignation of Noriko Shirota, a technical director of the Japanese Skating Federation. Ms. Shirota, a mentor to both skaters and their coaches, is said to have been responsible for building the country's skating empire. But when Katsuichiro Hisanaga, the former president of the federation and an ex–vice president of the ISU, was charged with embezzling federation funds, she was one of eight executive board members to step down. No charges were filed against Ms. Shirota, but she was criticized for her association with Mr. Hisanaga and for not being able to oversee the situation.

"The person who took Ms. Shirota's post and his associates are all new and inexperienced internationally," said an inside staff member who prefers to remain anonymous. "They won't be able to supervise the Japanese team like she did. Nobody has her knowledge or decision-making ability. She has given so much to skating in Japan, but after the scandal we are not even allowed to mention her name."

One piece of good news is that there will be a larger pool of figure skaters. Because skating is such a popular trend, every young girl wants to learn to skate. Every skating rink in Japan is packed with young kids. Shizuka Arakawa's childhood rink in Sendai was closed in late 2004 because of financial problems. But after her gold medal, thanks to the efforts of both local government and the private sector, the facility was able to reopen. We will see a generation of skaters who started to skate because they watched Miki Ando or Mao Asada.

In the figure skating world, where a 15-year-old sensation can reach overnight stardom, it may happen sooner than we think.

Yukina Ota

Johnny Weir

Glossary

AXEL

The most difficult jump, which is taken off from the front outside edge and is landed on the back outside edge of the opposite foot. Named for its inventor, Axel Paulsen, it is the only jump that is entered from a forward position; it therefore contains one half-revolution more than other jumps. A triple Axel, for instance, requires three-and-a-half revolutions of the body.

CAMEL SPIN

A spin done on one leg with the non-skating leg, or free leg, extended in the air in a position parallel to the ice.

CHOREOGRAPHY

An intentional, developed and/or original arrangement of all types of movements according to the principles of proportion, unity, space, pattern, structure and phrasing. Choreography is usually designed by a professional choreographer, who is often someone different from the skater's coach.

COMBINATION SPIN

The combination of several types of spins, in which the skater changes feet and position while maintaining speed throughout the spin.

COMPULSORY DANCE

The first stage of a dance competition. In most competitions, only one compulsory dance is performed, although some competitions require two. All couples perform the same selected dance to the same type of music. There is a set pattern for all couples, with required steps and holds; however, individual interpretations are permitted and encouraged.

CUP OF CHINA

The third Grand Prix event of the season. It replaced the Bofrost Cup (of Germany) in 2003.

CUP OF RUSSIA

The fifth event of the Grand Prix season. It began as the Moscow News Prize in 1972, making it the oldest Grand Prix event.

DEATH SPIRAL

A move in pair skating in which the man spins in a pivot position while holding one hand of his partner, who is spinning in a horizontal position with her body low and parallel to the ice.

EDGES

There is an inside edge (inner side of the foot) and an outside edge located on either side of the blade's grooved center. There is a forward and a backward for each edge, creating a total of four different edges.

ELIGIBLE SKATERS

The term used to define skaters who meet the requirements and follow the rules of U.S. Figure Skating and/or the ISU.

FLIP JUMP

A jump assisted by a toe pick, taken off from the back inside edge of one foot and landed on the back outside edge of the opposite foot.

FLYING CAMEL SPIN

A camel spin that is entered by leaping (or flying) into the pivot position directly from other skating motions.

FOOTWORK

A sequence of step maneuvers carrying the skater across the ice in patterns. It is intended to show the precision and dexterity of a skater's movements.

FREEDANCE

The third, final, and usually most important stage of a dance competition. The program is four minutes long, but can be 10 seconds longer or shorter. Couples are permitted to demonstrate a wide range of technical skills. There can be four lifts, one spin, one set of twizzles and other optional elements. The programs are usually dramatic and highly interpretive.

FREESKATE

The final segment of pairs and singles competition. The men's and pairs' programs are each four-and-a-half minutes long, while the women's program is four minutes long; each can be 10 seconds longer or shorter. Women are allowed a maximum of seven jump elements, while men may do eight. Only two of the six types of jumps may be repeated, and must be done in combination or in a jump sequence. Judges are looking for speed, technical execution, interpretation of music and theme, maximum ice coverage, and strong transition skills from element to element.

INTERNATIONAL JUDGING SYSTEM (IJS)

A radically changed scoring system adopted by the International Skating Union in 2004, now in use at all major international and domestic competitions. It replaced the old 6.0 scoring system, which was based on deductions from a maximum of 6.0 points and ordinals (placements) in each event. In the IJS, points are awarded for technical evaluation of elements in the performance (roughly equivalent to the former "technical" mark) and for five additional components (roughly equivalent to the old "artistic" mark). Those additional components are: skating skills; transitions; performance; composition and interpretation. In ice dance, a sixth component, timing, is added. Points earned for each segment of the competition are added up and the skater with the most points wins. Unlike the old 6.0 system, judges in international events are now protected by anonymity.

INTERNATIONAL SKATING UNION (ISU)

The worldwide organizing body for figure skating. The ISU is recognized by the International Olympic Committee as the sanctioning body for all figure skating competitions, rules, procedures and Olympic eligibility.

LAYBACK SPIN

A spin in an upright position with the head and shoulders pushed backwards, and the back arched. Usually performed by women.

LIFT

A move in pairs skating in which the man lifts his partner above his head, arms fully extended. It contains moves and changes of position on the way up, on the way down, and in rotation.

LOOP JUMP

A jump not assisted by a toe pick, taken off from the back outside edge and landed on the back outside edge of the same foot. It is noticeable for its backward glide and wide curve.

LUTZ JUMP

A jump assisted by a toe pick, taken off from the back outside edge and landed on the back outside edge of the opposite foot. Named for its first practitioner, Alois Lutz.

NHK TROPHY

The last of the six events on the Grand Prix circuit. Held in Japan, it began in 1981. After the NHK is completed, the top points-earners from the circuit earn places in the Grand Prix Final.

ORIGINAL DANCE

The second stage of a dance competition. All couples skate to the same rhythm, within a required range of tempo, but create an original version of that style of dance. The character of the on-ice dance must be retained from its ballroom version and must contain two short lifts, one dance-spin and two kinds of step sequences. The program is two minutes and 30 seconds long, but can be 10 seconds longer or shorter.

REFEREE

The official at a competition who has full authority over every skating aspect of the event and is the chairperson for the panel of judges.

SALCHOW

A jump not assisted by a toe pick, taken off from the back inside edge of one foot and landed on the back outside edge of the other foot. Named for early world champion Ulrich Salchow.

SHORT PROGRAM

The first segment of competition for single and pairs skaters. The short program consists of eight required moves or elements performed to music, and can be no longer than two minutes and 50 seconds. For singles there are three jump elements (one of them a combination jump), three spins, and two step-sequences (footwork), done in any order. In pairs, the required elements include two different types of lifts, a throw jump, side-by-side double or triple jumps, solo spins, a pairs spin, a death spiral and a spiral step sequence.

SKATE AMERICA

The opening event of the Grand Prix season. Its first year was 1979, in Lake Placid.

SKATE CANADA (THE EVENT)

The second stop on the Grand Prix circuit, usually held around the last week of October. It began at Calgary in 1973 — making it the second oldest of all Grand Prix events.

SKATE CANADA (THE ORGANIZATION)

The body that oversees figure skating development, training, competition and national teams in Canada. It has 125,000 regular members and nearly 200,000 overall. As Canada's representative member of the International Skating Union, Skate Canada administers ISU policies and rules in Canada.

SPIRAL

A move in which a skater demonstrates flexibility and a fluid line by extending the non-skating leg back and into the air during a long glide.

STEP SEQUENCE

A sequence of choreographically related steps that immediately follow one another, executed in time to the music.

THROW JUMP

An important move in pairs skating in which the man assists (throws) the woman into the air — where she rotates — and then lands, going in a backward direction. The different throw jumps are named for the singles jumps that use the same takeoff and landing edges (as in throw triple Salchow).

TOE PICKS

The teeth at the front of the skate blade, used primarily to assist with jumping and spinning.

TROPHÉE ERIC BOMPARD

Held in France, it is the fourth event of the Grand Prix season. It began in 1987 as Grand Prix International de Paris (and later, Trophée Lalique).

TWIZZLE

A traveling turn on one foot with one or more rotations, quickly executed with a continuous (uninterrupted) action.

U.S. FIGURE SKATING

The national organizing body for figure skating in the United States. As the country's representative to the ISU, U.S. Figure Skating develops and supervises all levels of skating within the U.S. and administers ISU policies and rules in the country. Total membership has reached close to 200,000, although more than 130,000 members are in the basic skills (learn-to-skate) programs.

Index

Acknowledgments

To Gérard for the absolutely stunning images; you are a true artist. To Steve, Dan, Michael and Barb at Firefly for their vision, professionalism and expertise. And to, as always, my inner circle: Jess, Toby, Mom and Michelle, for their belief and inspiration.

STEVE MILTON

To my wife Doreen, for her kind and patient support which keeps me going when, sometimes, I think I cannot! To Firefly books for their superb publishing spirit. To Steve Milton for always having the right word and to Akiko Tamura for her smart perspective on such a wonderful sport. Finally, to all the skaters and to the New Wave which has already defined higher standards and continues to push on! It is great to be with you, and you are forever an inspiration.

GÉRARD CHÂTAIGNEAU